Odyssey of a Texas Sailor

The true story of a country boy's dream to sail solo across the Atlantic Ocean.

by Drew Paige

with John H. Clark III

johnclarkbooks

Dedication

Tucked inside an old, black, weather-worn satchel beside a desk, covered in aerial maps, lay the personal hand-written accounts of Dean Drew Meeks, the Texas Sailor. This private collection of notes remained dormant for close to thirty years, untouched while the storyteller was alive. Written on yellow note pads – now a little brown from time – were unbelievable tales of adventure, desperation, reflections, love, fear, and most of all, courage. It is my hope to bring this epic journey, this odyssey, to life.

My name is Drew Meeks Paige. I am the youngest daughter of Dean and Margaret Meeks, and I inherited the black weathered satchel, the desk, and the ranch where a large majority of the dreams described in this book were formed.

Since undertaking this project to have these journals published, I have been on my own unexpected adventure. The original goal was to type up the hand-written notes and put them in a binder for friends and family. I never imagined that I would be adding my own input, re-living childhood memories, and gathering tales from friends and family. Many hours were spent researching locations, learning nautical terms, and verifying spelling – which I found to be a waste of time because Dad didn't misspell anything, except maybe the name of one of the Nazi prison camps.

Actually, he didn't really misspell that – he put down the first letters and left a blank to be filled in at a later date. If there *are* any misspelled words, please blame that on my below-par typing skills.

Odyssey of a Texas Sailor is dedicated first and foremost to Dean Drew Meeks. It is his tale; his adventure; his writings, which have inspired the book. Secondly, this book is in honor of my mother, his wife for fifty years, Margaret Lynn Meeks. She was the wind in his sails. Not only is this a great adventure; it is a kind of love story that is rare in today's world.

I would also like to thank and acknowledge John Clark, who I met through a series of "God winks." John has given me direction and encouragement to write. Without John being placed in my path,

I believe this story would still be sitting in binders on that aerial map-covered desk. With his direction, I was able to explore my own writing. It has been a privilege and an honor to work with John.

Finally, the most unexpected gift I have received from all this has been healing. I encourage everyone to write. Your children will appreciate your writings long after you are gone.

Table of Contents

Introduction

A lot of people dream big dreams, but that's as far as it ever goes. Big dreams.

Not Dean Drew Meeks.

A lifelong resident of rural central Texas, Meeks was a talented athlete, father, husband, pilot, prankster, rancher, soldier, and sailor who set out to at least try and turn every dream he ever had into reality.

When he decided to pursue a love of airplanes and flying, the former U.S. Army paratrooper took lessons and bought himself a small Cessna. He customized his beloved new plane from a two-seater into a makeshift four-seater, so he could take his wife and two daughters for rides, which often included loop-the-loop acrobatics, landing on a two-lane asphalt roadway near the house, and parking the plane in the front yard.

A lifelong fondness of water he developed as a boy learning to swim in the cool creeks of Coryell County led Meeks to buy a 21-foot sailboat and haul it over to nearby Lake Belton. From there, it was hit-or-miss, sink-or-swim – sometimes nearly literally – as he read books on sailing and taught himself to navigate the mostly calm lake waters, before graduating to testing his skills further south on Galveston Bay.

When his youngest daughter, Drew, joined the U.S. Air Force, was stationed in England, and got married, Dean went over for a visit. He wanted to see his little girl, of course, but there was also another reason for the trip:

"After they were back in England, setting up housekeeping in a small, cold, farm cottage on the banks of the river, Little Ouse, a plan began forming in my mind," Meeks wrote in his journal. "Using their homestead as a launching point for an adventure long stored in the cluttered-up attic of my mind, why couldn't I – a self-taught, proven sailor of fresh water lakes – purchase a craft in England, sail

1

it back to Houston, and make a handsome profit on its resale at that oil-rich port?"

And so it began – what would become the biggest adventure of the 49-year-old adventurer's life.

Meeks tells the tale himself in a highly entertaining day-by-day written account that begins with him questioning, if not his sanity, then at the very least his decision-making faculties as he and his boat are pounded and pummeled in pitch-black darkness by heavy waves and wind off the coast of Spain:

"How in the ever-loving, blue-eyed world did a part-time rancher and jack of all trades (master of none) from arid central Texas get himself into the Atlantic Ocean off the coast of Europe on a night like this?" Meeks wrote. "Well, if anyone is to blame, it's the guy aboard this sloop, rolled in a tarp, lashed to the bulkhead, gritting his teeth."

Follow along as Meeks recounts the fascinating story of not only finding his dream vessel, "White Swan," and setting sail from the English Channel, but also the charming memories of his carefree childhood years and the events that helped shape his life and eventually led to his remarkable journey to sail the high seas.

Along with a word-for-word transcript of Meeks' original journal, this story includes an assortment of additional memories from Drew (*in italics*), who lovingly preserved her dad's writings, the newspaper clippings about his voyage and life, and never gave up her own quest to share it all with the world.

Everyone has big dreams. Unfortunately, for one reason or another, not everyone sees those dreams come true.

What is your big dream?

Has it come true?

Will it come true?

What will it take to make it happen?

Read and be inspired by the story of a simple man from Texas who somehow had what it takes to turn his dreams into reality.

2

Chapter One

Beyond this place, there be Dragons!

In the pitch-black darkness, the Swan rolled hard over on her port side, lurching as her stern rose to meet the giant wave, take its measure, then straightened herself in its wake. HAL, the automatic tiller I had purchased in England, strained in protest as it attempted to correct the yaw of the vessel before the next wave made its onslaught. Already, this had been a long night and yet it was only a few minutes past midnight. It's hard to get any sleep with your jaw locked and your teeth gritting, wondering if the next wave will break over into the cockpit and soak any dry spot that still remained on your tired, cold, tense, body.

I knew I should claw my way out of my makeshift nest to check for lights from either the shore or other boats that might be out on this God forsaken night. But I also knew that it had taken a long time to acquire the small amount of warmth and comfort that I now enjoyed, wedged forward in the cockpit, half under the splash guard that protected the hatchway. In boots and rain gear, I had managed to work my tired body into my sleeping bag, insert my feet and legs into the jib's waterproof sail bag, then finally wrap a small square of canvas over my head and upper body.

Snug in this semi-dry cocoon, I then lashed myself with a line to the cabin bulkhead, taking a couple of dallies around my wrist and leaving the rope in my hand for a quick release in case of an emergency. With my body wedged and lashed in this position, I could remain somewhat stable as the Swan rolled, lurched, and bucked, running before a stiff wind somewhere off the coast of northern Spain.

How in the ever-loving blue-eyed world did a part-time rancher and jack of all trades (master of none) from arid central Texas get himself into the Atlantic Ocean off the coast of Europe on a night like this? Well if anyone is to blame, it's the guy aboard this sloop rolled in a tarp, lashed to the bulkhead, gritting his teeth.

But then again, maybe I'm not solely to blame.

What about those shifty people from the National Geographic Society who kept sending me those yellow magazines in their plain brown wrappers, filled with stories of teenage sailors who circumnavigated the globe alone, or maybe with a cat? And their supplemental maps, modern and up-to-date on one side, while historic on the other, with routes of the famous explorers boldly crossing oceans never before traversed. How was a dreamer like me supposed to resist the temptation to tag along? To me, the grass on the far side of the fence has always looked greener.

And the oh-so helpful librarians in my hometown of Gatesville who were so willing to help me locate Michener's "Tales of the South Pacific," or some book by Melville that brought the smell of salt spray to your nostrils when you opened it. Yes, these cunning people also helped me along the primrose path, leading to the voyage of the Swan and the cold, miserable niche of the universe that my tired body occupied at present.

Thump! The Swan shuddered as a giant wave caught her just right, slammed hard against the stern and broke over the splash boards, half filling the cockpit and completely filling my makeshift bunk. The self-bailing cockpit would be dry again in a few minutes, but my sleeping bag would be wet for days. Seemed like a good time to get up before too much cold water found its way into my foul weather gear and underwear.

After pushing my soggy bedroll through the hatch down into the cabin below, I braced myself and surveyed the wild night and sea that surrounded me. A light rain pushed by the hard-north wind stung my face when I looked north. There were no lights from shoreward at all. I estimated my position to be twenty to twenty-five miles off the northern Spanish coast, running parallel to it.

Off the starboard bow, maybe ten miles out, I could see the lights of a large tanker heading south in its designated sea lane, bound for the Mediterranean or Africa or somewhere. Wouldn't it be

4

nice to be aboard it, in a nice warm bunk and be able to sleep soundly until daybreak, then wake to a good hot meal and an extra hot coffee!

This was no time for daydreaming. The wind was getting stronger and the waves getting higher. If I intended to get any rest this night, the working jib must be pulled down and replaced by the storm jib, a small triangle sail of reinforced canvas that would take a lot of pressure off the rudder, the vessel, and me.

Using a flashlight, I worked my way down through the cabin, then forward to the sail locker. In the semi-darkness, with the Swan rolling and bucking, this could be compared with a trip through the "crazy house" at a carnival. Nothing is stable, the bulkhead comes hard against your head or the deck drops from beneath your feet, then comes up quickly and tries to stack you in a corner.

Back on deck with the storm jib and a strong flashlight, I attached a line to my safety harness and began carefully working my way forward in the darkness, moving between swells and bracing myself at the crest. At the base of the mast, I tied my light to shine in the general direction of the foredeck, which was often awash. Loosening the jib halyard, I lowered the working jib, gathering it in as it came down to keep it from being blown overboard. If the theory of evolution is indeed a fact, by this point in history sailors should have developed at least two more arms and hands to do the work that has to be done while holding on for dear life!

After lashing the jib to the leeward rail, I attached the storm jib to the forestay and the jib halyard to the sail, hauling it up smartly and making it fast. As I was about to congratulate myself on a hard job well done under difficult circumstances, the deck dropped from beneath my feet. That law of gravity sent my prostrate body in hot pursuit only to be met by the deck as it returned upon the next swell. With bruised ribs, no breath, and sea water gushing into the seat of my foul weather britches, I realized that indeed, this could be a very long night.

Chapter Two

I have always liked to play in water.

An aunt of mine is fond of telling (and telling) about the time I stayed a while with her when I was very young. It seems that after being scrubbed and rubbed and decked out in my finest little Sunday-go-to-meeting suit, I climbed back into the old tin tub when her back was turned. And apparently, if there be any truth to this tale, I repeated this performance after being dried and re-dressed. She's never said, when telling the story, whether I received a spanking or not, but if I did, it didn't seem to deter me from getting into hot water quite often the rest of my life.

One of my favorite places to play when I was very young, and still one of my favorite places, is Hood Spring, near the banks of the Dodds Creek, about fifty yards from the house in which I was born. There my brother, my cousins, and I entertained ourselves catching "minners," crawdads, tadpoles, and poison ivy.

The macho thing there was to see who could dangle the largest crawfish from his earlobe, without tears coming to his eyes. For this feat of bravery, a pint jar of spring water was handy by the dangler, and when the pain became unbearable or he was declared the winner, he dipped the danglee (the crawdad) in the jar. The crawdad, thinking he was back in the spring, released his pincher hold, allowing the participant in this game to emerge with only a slightly damaged ear.

It wasn't long before we migrated on down to Dodds Creek and the Dyson hole. Now this was a real body of water, over your head and hands in the deepest spot and spring-fed cold. This famous swimming hole was named after my aunt Twink's mother, who was a tenacious fisher person and a full sister to Job, of biblical fame.

She would sit for hours and days on that high north bank, fishing for perch and denying our parched bodies the cool water of our favorite swimming hole. We thought she was ancient, with her long dress, field bonnet, wrinkled sun-browned face, and snapping black eyes. She must have been around fifty years old though, as she died a couple years ago, at the age of a hundred and two. Fifty doesn't seem that old to me now ...

~~~~

"Daddy was a great swimmer," daughter, Drew, says, "and was drawn to the water like a moth to a flame. I remember many summers spent after a hard day's work playing in the Dodds creek, or some other watering hole he knew of. We would travel to Tankawa Park, Lake Belton and many others. On longer trips, we would travel to Lake Buchanan or Inks Lake, and Galveston was one of our favorite summer vacation spots. We didn't sleep in a hotel, but on the beach in a tent. I have the same love for the water as Dad.

"In a recent conversation with cousin Ranzell Meeks, I learned how my dad came to be a swimmer. There were six, sometimes seven boys that ran the banks of the Dodds creek. Ranzell was one of them, and Dean was another. There was Weldon Meeks (dad's older brother), cousins Dewy Meeks, Robert Earl Meeks (known as Bleachy), another cousin, Royce Pennington, and good family friend, Norris Sexton.

"Since dad was the youngest by two to three years, he was the last to learn to swim. While he was old enough to run with the others but not old enough to swim, they were forbidden to go to the creek without an adult. They were instructed that they could not go to the creek until Dean knew how to swim. So, they would sneak off to the creek and play, trying to be quiet enough so that no one would know where they were. One day, they decided they needed to teach Dean to swim so that their restrictions on the creek could be lifted.

"They would put Dean on a board and he would float and paddle all over the creek. Then one day he just swam right off the board and was swimming with the others. Now, they had a dilemma.

"Dean could swim, but if the folks found out, then the boys would be in trouble for taking him to the creek without permission. One day, after Dean had been swimming a bit, the Dodds creek boys *forgot to keep their voices down. They were having a grand time at their favorite swimming hole, the Dyson hole. (Where it got its name is another story).*

"Anyway, as Ranzell tells it, they were jumping off the banks and just playing as hard as young boys can play, and it wasn't long before my granddad, Manson, could no longer pretend he didn't know where they were. So, he stopped what he was doing (milking cows and general dairyman work) and went to the creek.

"When he arrived, all the boys were on the high banks of the creek and all their clothes were on the other side. Manson scolded them for coming to the creek before Dean could swim. He told them to get their clothes and come home for their punishment.

"So, all the boys, Dean included, jumped in the creek and swam to the other side to fetch their clothes. When Manson, or Poi as we called him, saw that Dean could swim, he just shook his head and told them to keep playing. Obviously, their creek restrictions had been rescinded."

~~~~

Cousin Royce, now a Baptist preacher, will always stand out in my mind for his feats of daring at the Dyson hole. He wasn't the best swimmer and couldn't stay underwater any longer than anyone else, but on the rope swing he set a record that may never be broken.

We would swing out over the stream, turn loose and dive, flip, or cannonball yelling, "Geronimo!" and scream to get all the attention we could. Some of the boys, me not included, being two or three years younger than the rest, had managed to perfect the "flip and a half" and naturally began talking about doing a complete "double flip." We figured it would take a powerful swing to get high enough to pull that off.

Cousin Royce, always up to a challenge, screwed up his courage and decided to go for it. Someone, (Bleachy) held the swing for him high up on the bank while he got a run to build up speed. Here he came! Grabbing the swing, he fairly zoomed out over the water. At the highest point of the arc, he released, did a perfect double somersault, and landed flat on his back on the far bank! After he came to, he was declared the winner, and no one ever tried to challenge his record, which still stands.

Daddy was as big a kid as any of us and though he worked long hours a day and seven days a week, he usually had time to hammer us out an old flat-bottomed creek boat which we mentally transformed into a pirate schooner or a sleek Viking raider. His stories of shipping out on a coal ship from Port Arthur to New York during the depression didn't do anything to dampen my enthusiasm for the sea, either.

Somewhere around 1950, a few of the cousins were in college, and the others were getting their higher education in Korea. My new running buddy and best friend was new to this area and lived a couple of miles up the creek at a farm called, "Chick town," where there used to be a hatchery.

One Saturday morning, in the fall of the year after heavy rains had pushed the roaring creek out of its banks, I proceeded to teach my friend, C.F., the fine art of roping and riding logs down the rampage to an old iron bridge at the bottom of our place, a distance of about three miles.

Some of the rapids were pretty hectic and you sure didn't want to get caught in any barbed wire from the washed-out water gaps. Other than keeping a close eye out for irritated cottonmouth water moccasins, it was, as they now say, a piece of cake. The first trip down was successful, with only minor bruises and briar cuts that wouldn't hurt until we warmed up anyway, so we trekked across country to his place and tried it again. This run also went very well until the very end, then it took a nasty turn.

A car was stopped in the middle of the iron bridge, and C.F.'s mother was standing at the rail. She had a funny look in her eyes, and her face was white as a sheet. We swam ashore and climbed the muddy bank with some misgivings. "Junior!" she said to C.F., "get in the car!" Then she stared at me. I looked everywhere else but at her – you could tell she was really mad.

"Young man, do you want me to take you home?" she said.

9

"No ma'am, it's not far, and I'd just as soon walk." I said.

She continued to stare at me a long time while I concentrated on getting the mud out from between my toes. I didn't know what C.F. had done to disturb his mother this much. It must have been something he did before I came over, because I had been with him all morning and hadn't even heard him say a cuss word. I wanted to tell her this, but something told me I'd be better off if I stayed very quiet, which I did until they drove away.

Dodds Creek boys

10

Chapter Three

If there is a common denominator in male human beings, it is probably the dream of sailing away to the South Seas, escaping all responsibility, and living a life of leisure in the warm tropics; never disturbed by the alarm clock or the 6 o'clock news, or the April 16th deadline for filing the hated income tax return.

The more years spent farming and ranching in the hot, dry, dusty central Texas area, the stronger the dream becomes, until at times a person with a wild imagination can see the sails and the tall ships riding the heat waves across the hayfield in front of his tractor. It was during one of these times, astride a hot tractor, that I decided I couldn't possibly live any longer without a sailboat.

We found the "Sard,"* a trailered, twenty-one-foot sloop, tucked away in the classified ads of the Waco Tribune Herald and bought her on the spot. The previous owner's dreams of sailing the high seas had to be set aside and replaced temporarily with need to convert the two-car garage into a bedroom for a fast-growing family. They had set two anchors, a girl and a boy.

* Sara was the name of the first grandchild born in 1984, and somehow this slang for Sara – "Sard" – was the name of this first sailboat.

Now this little fiberglass sloop of ours would probably only draw amused glances and remarks of "how cute" in the major sailing ports of the world, and certainly not be invited to join the sophisticated yacht clubs. But in land-locked Gatesville, twenty miles from the nearest lake, why she was the grandest – and possibly the only – sailing craft about. I began to think of myself in terms of "Captain Meeks," and my wife Margaret as, "First Mate." She was quick to point out that there would be no "Second Mate."

I was very anxious to launch Sard into the dark waters of Lake Belton, but my crew was, at the time, not seaworthy – Margaret having recently had major abdominal surgery, and I still had my arm in a cast after a wrist operation to replace a worn-out bone with a green plastic replica.

So, for a few days, I had to content myself with prowling the decks and reading every "How to Sail" book I could lay my hands on at the half-priced bookstore in Waco.

Finally, I could stand it no longer.

I convinced Margaret that if she would help, she would have to do nothing more strenuous than to mind the tiller and soak up the sunshine, while I tended to the sails. After all, sailing is very easy, and I had read all the books. Well, not quite all the books. I do remember seeing, a year later, in a shop window in St. Peter's port on the Isle of Guernsey in the Channel Islands, a book that I had possibly missed. I don't remember the title but prominent on the dust cover was the definition of sailing: "The art of staying wet and ill while going nowhere at great expense." Truer words, outside the Bible, were never written.

For our maiden voyage aboard the "Sard," we trailered her to Belton Lake, a distance of twenty miles, and with a crew of cripples, proceeded to make her lake worthy. Getting the mast stepped and launching the boat was quite a chore for a one-armed captain with a gimpy crew, but it was finally accomplished.

We used the outboard motor to get to the middle of the lake, where I attached the rudder and ran up the main sail and jib. With Margaret at the tiller, we tacked back and forth across the wind while I got the feel of changing the sails with each tack. Noticing that we were making quite a bit of leeway toward the rocky shoreline, I asked Margaret to point her up into the wind.

Something was wrong.

According to the book, we should be clawing off, but my eyes told me we were getting disastrously close to some large boat-eating rocks! I took the tiller and came about on a port tack, but we didn't improve our situation at all. A little light bulb came on over my head, and the sarcastic voice of one of the Irish Sea captains of my readings said, "Aye, and she won't be sailing up into the wind if you've not lowered your keel board, now will she lad?" The keel board!

"You damn fool!" I yelled at myself, as I stumbled forward to drop both sails. There was no time to crank down the keel and barely enough time to get my body overboard to be used as a fender to keep my precious sloop off the jagged shore. There I was, a one-armed, would-be sailor overboard, trying to keep my boat off the rocks while a stiff breeze and choppy waves did their best to pile her up on that rocky beach. It was a Mexican standoff. And no place to go.

"What can I do?" Margaret's anxious voice called from the cockpit.

"You could have married a smarter man!" I muttered to myself.

Anyway, to make an embarrassing story shorter. I did a little nautical dance between my sloop and disaster while my first mate, by various signals, gained the assistance of a couple of somewhat amused fisherman in a motorboat. After a tow to the middle of the lake, accompanied by what seemed to me rather over-wide grins from our benefactors, I set out again to transfer my "book learning" to practical application, this time with the aid of a lowered keel.

It made quite a difference.

~~~~

"I was stationed in England with the U.S. Air Force in the early '80s," Drew explained, "and at the time, Dad was reading every book about sailing he could get his hands on. I guess he read all he thought he needed, because next I heard, he had a boat!

"I wish I had paid more attention when he told me this story, but on his maiden voyage, there was 'trouble with the help.'

"Mom had just had a hysterectomy and was not to do any strenuous activities, and I believe he had just had some type of hand surgery. They were a crippled crew, to say the least. From what I remember, mother was demanding that he put her off on land 'right here,' and he was incapable of maneuvering the boat anywhere, much less 'right here.'

13

"That should have ended his sailing career, but I believe it just encouraged it. He continued to teach himself to sail in the calm waters of Lake Belton. There were also some sailing trips in Galveston Bay, but nothing compared to his greatest adventure."

Chapter Four

Probably the main catalyst in helping me convert my wondering dreams into partial reality was my youngest daughter, Drew Anne, although I'm sure this was not her intent.

Drew is a very bright, outgoing girl who after the restrictions of home and high school, proceeded to enjoy herself immensely at a very small college about eighty miles from our home. It was understood from the beginning that although we heartily approved of her pursuit of higher education and would help some, she would have to work to pay most of her own expenses.

This was no problem as both our daughters excelled at any work they undertook. Drew and her older sister, Andrea, were experienced ranch hands by the time they reached their teens, being able to handle horses, cattle, and all the rough and tumble work involved in "working the calves."

In high school, both took up working with the older folks in the local rest home and were really proud to be paid the minimum wage of $3.25 an hour, as this was considerably more than they received from me for working with the livestock.

At college, Drew seemed to divide her time between whatever job she held, and a social organization known as the OWLS, whose major function it seemed to me, was promoting dances, parties, pranks, and chili cook-offs. Needless to say, with a small amount of time also used for sleeping, this left very few hours of each day devoted to academic excellence.

Drew totaled up her hours and grade points after two years of this hectic pace, determined she would be a long time graduating, and decided she needed more structure in her life. So, after much testing, some waiting, and a going away party or two, it was off to the U.S. Air Force to become an aircraft electrical systems specialist.

Being a lot like me, upon enlisting she had volunteered for overseas duty in the Philippines, probably with visions of beautiful islands, palm trees, and sunny beaches. Characteristically, the military decided she would best fit into their scheme of things in the damp, cold, rain-swept fens of eastern England, promptly posting her to Mildenhall Air Base.

I don't know how Drew felt about this, but her parents were very relieved, as this was about the time the Marcos government was being overthrown, and Imelda was packing all her shoes for a quick trip to Hawaii.

At Mildenhall, Drew quickly became proficient at trouble-shooting, locating and repairing shorts in the maze of wiring that makes up the electrical systems of the KC–135, the Air Force's main air-to-air refueling tanker.

As a cheerleader for the base football team, she soon caught the eye, or he hers, of a young man on the team from San Antonio, and it wasn't long before they were flying back to central Texas to be looked over by the future in-laws, approved of, and married.

After they were back in England, setting up housekeeping in a small, cold, farm cottage on the banks of the River Little Ouse, a plan began forming in my mind – using their homestead as a launching point for an adventure long stored in the cluttered-up attic of my mind.

Why couldn't I – a self-taught, proven sailor of fresh water lakes – purchase a craft in England, sail it back to Houston, and make a handsome profit on its resale at that oil-rich port?

While the economy of England was in somewhat of a recession at the time, the U.S. dollar was very strong and pushing close to the value of the pound sterling. I had no trouble at all convincing myself that this was a fine undertaking and immediately set about proving its practicality to my long-suffering wife, Margaret. Probably the greatest obstacle to overcome would be convincing her (that) there was no truth at all to that old adage about sailors having "a girl in every port!"

Finances shouldn't be a cause of any friction between us as she and I had long ago split the blanket on money matters. For years, I had labored under the chauvinistic attitude that if the man of the house didn't maintain firm control of the family finances, the entire world economy would immediately collapse. Margaret had somewhat grudgingly gone along with this arrangement until – after earning a college degree in social studies and securing a very good job – she decided she should tend to her own finances.

I reminded her how I had always been very fair and divided the excess money after the bills were paid, hoping she would do the same. My wife remembered things somewhat differently, maintaining there had never been any excess money to divide. Finally, we settled upon an arrangement where, after the household bills were split somewhat evenly, it was every man for himself and the devil be damned!

Though not being wildly impressed with my plan to sail off across some strange ocean, she did agree to "sort of" look after the cattle for me while I was gone, and perhaps fix a water gap or two in case we got any summer rains. My neighbor and good friend, Gene Chitwood, though not actually volunteering to do any hard work, said he would help keep an eye on the place. I think Dianne, his wife, resigned herself to consoling the grieving widow after my failure to return.

At the National Bank in Gatesville, they agreed to help finance my venture if I located a boat that suited my purposes, only requiring that I put up my small herd of cattle as collateral and carry life insurance on the note. This just suited me fine, for I figured those old cows would never know their survival depended upon my safe return.

Things now began to move faster, much as a sluggish old muddy river does as it nears a cataract, growing swift and loud, eliminating any chance of turning back. Old time-worn, hazy day dreams that I had been comfortable with all my life began to solidify into some sort of nervous reality – exhilarating, but a little scary, too. It was time to go.

After packing some sturdy clothes, I said my goodbyes, hugged my loved ones, and headed for Houston in my beat-up old pickup truck.

Along the back roads of Coryell County and central Texas, it is customary to acknowledge an oncoming motorist with a smile and a slight wave of the hand, whether you recognize them or not. As it often takes both hands firmly clenched to the steering wheel to avoid a collision or sliding off a narrow caliche road into the ditch, the art of waving has, over the years, been modified to simply raising the index finger and a nod of the head.

There are, however, some variations. A close friend is usually greeted with a big smile and a hearty wave of the left arm out of the open window, sometimes accompanied by a long honk on the horn. If you have had serious problems with the person in the approaching pickup truck, such as trespassing livestock or heated political differences, you simply stare straight ahead as if the road were empty. This snub, more often than not, is answered in kind.

On the three-hour drive to Houston, certain changes in highway customs readily became apparent. Traveling speeds pick up considerably on the major highways between larger towns and waving to each oncoming vehicle is just too hard on the wrist. Still, the driving is friendly, with most folks willing to help another motorist pass on these crowded roads.

The 610 loop around Houston, though, is a whole new ballgame.

Speeds took another jump to about twenty miles per hour over the posted limit, and home-loving, God-fearing Houstonians became crazed stock car racers, as they hurled themselves down the expressway. It is something like the Indianapolis 500, except there are a lot more cars.

Staying under the speed limit would be suicidal, and using common courtesy, say to drop back to let someone change lanes, is viewed as a weakness or just downright weird. I did, however, at times notice that a few of these wild-eyed drivers used the country custom of greeting other motorists, except that they used a different finger.

Bumper to bumper, door to door, at eighty miles an hour, this mass of metal whirls around the city at probably four revolutions per hour. Some drivers, though, have to pull off to refuel and "re-nerve," their positions instantly filled by fresh would-be Mario Andrettis bent on setting new records for the Houston 610.

I am not sure how many times I circled the city before managing to extricate myself from this runaway centrifuge somewhere in the south of the city near the airport.

C.F. Lively, my old friend from the Chicktown farm on the Dodd's Creek, was now a successful builder and developer in this area. So, after mooching a meal off of his wife, Beverly, and him, I deposited my old truck in their driveway and persuaded Carey, as he now called himself, to drive me to the airport.

I thought this a very friendly gesture, seeing as how many years earlier I had accidentally shot a hole through the calf of his leg with a .22 rifle while on a skunk hunt. Even though I bandaged his leg with my old muddy sock, he managed to live anyway, but that's another story.

Chapter Five

Ever since I took my first plane ride in an old cloth-covered Piper Cub back in the mid-1940s, I have been hooked on airplanes and airports. For twenty years, I owned a 1946 Cessna 120, a very tough, very forgiving little airplane that got me into and out of many tight scrapes. I even own an ultra-lite aircraft, but I keep it dismantled and locked up for my safety.

Having lots of time to kill at Houston's Hobby airfield, I would have liked to stroll around among the planes and mingle with the mechanics and service personnel. But, as bomb threats and Libyan-backed hijacking was peaking at this time, I figured I would probably be unwelcome on the tarmac.

I had even been cautioned before leaving Gatesville that if I happened to meet my brother-in-law, Jack Pardee, on the flight to New York, I should be careful and not greet him with a loud, "Hi, Jack!"

~~~

"Dean Meeks was the type of man that when he put his mind to do something, he did it," daughter, Drew, recalls. "He loved airplanes and flying. Though on a small income, he took flying lessons and became a pilot.

"He bought a small Cessna 120 tail-dragger. This was a two-seater airplane, which he converted into a four-seater for my sister and me. We rode in the back, and he and mama rode in the front. I can remember flying with him and he would do the loops where there was nothing between you and the ground but the seat belt and the window.

"We would land and take off at the small Gatesville airport, and mama would drive us home. Dad, on the other hand, would land the plane on Levita Road, in front of the house, and pull into the front yard to park. Not everyone had an airplane in their front yard.

"Once, he told us that he needed our largest doll, and we wanted to know why. He said that he was going to fill her full of rocks and strap his parachute on her and throw her out of the plane to see if his chute still worked.

"He had been a paratrooper in the Army, and he planned to do one last jump on his 40th birthday.

"When he wasn't jumping out of airplanes, he was playing football all over Europe with the Army team. From what I was told, it was some of the roughest, toughest football around. Newspaper articles called him the 'tall Texan' when he played.

"He played high school football and college ball at Texas A&M, under the legendary coach, Bear Bryant, but dropped out of college in his third year and joined the military.

"It was difficult to get the reason out of him, and that reason was not exposed until his funeral. He was a man that if he did not have something good to say about someone, then he didn't. When asked about playing football under Bear Bryant, he never had anything to say. I asked his mother one day if she knew why he had dropped out of college and joined the army. She told me what she knew.

"According to the story that she received, she said that he had been dropped from the team after a game when he had not performed his best. He was running a fever of 103 degrees and was not allowed to sit out of the game. He told her that he played even though sick and was dropped from the team.

"I later found that was not the truth, or not the whole truth.

"At my dad's funeral, his brother-in-law, Jack Pardee (the well-known professional football player and coach), shared with us what really transpired.

"Jack said that Dean was lined up against that year's Heisman trophy winner, and that it was a rough game. The Aggies won, and all were to sit together as a team to dine after the game. For some reason, maybe the sickness, or maybe because he was lined up against one of the best – or maybe both – Dean was told to not sit with the team. Apparently, if you did not perform up to the standards of the coaches, you could not eat with the team.

21

"That was the last day he played ball under Coach Bear Bryant.

"He packed his bags and signed on the dotted line for a new adventure in the United States Army. Jack went on to say that Bear Bryant was later quoted as saying, "We didn't do that Meeks boy right!"

"So, dad spent some time in the Army, in Europe, played football while stationed in Germany, and jumped out of a few perfectly good airplanes, too. He married Margaret between college and Germany, and she met up with him there, where they started their married life in a land far from their Central Texas roots.

"And he never did make that last jump on his birthday. He did test the chute by throwing the doll out of the plane somewhere near the house. The chute opened just fine, and the doll landed.

"My grandfather, Manson, was waiting on the ground, and he followed the doll and chute. When it landed, he hurried out in the pasture and lay on the ground. When someone came along to see who was jumping out of planes on Levita Road, my granddad got up and dusted himself off like he had just landed.

"The doll did not survive the jump, and I think my mother was not quite ready to lose her husband in an airplane jump, so she hid the chute, and my dad never found it.

"Life was never boring on the dairy."

~~~~

Having often been told that I was easily entertained, I stretched myself out on a lounge chair, pushed my hat down 'til it nearly covered my eyes, and got into some serious people watching. For this sport, air terminals are where the major league playoffs are held. At no other place will you see so many strange people doing so many strange things, with maybe the possible exception of that bunch of crazies that get together in Terlingua, down on the Rio Grande, for the world's championship chili cook off.

Over in a corner with a roped-off section, there were a bunch of chairs with small individual pay television sets, mounted on each of them. The occupants of the chairs stared straight into the little flickering boxes with dazed gloomy-eyed looks on their faces. I finally figured out that these were TV addicts that were being separated from the tube for the first time and must get a quick fix to keep from being completely drawn back into reality.

Although there wasn't much going on here, at the Newark terminal the next day, we weary travelers were treated to a show that we should have had to pay to see. Ahead of me in line, a young couple, possibly Italian and very hip in their modern dress, were having trouble getting through the metal detector. The girl wore black stretch pants and an oversize white shirt that came nearly to her knees. The shirt was gathered at the waist by a black patent leather belt with a gold-colored metal buckle, possibly as big as a dinner plate. Although she had shucked most of her jewelry and given up her huge purse, the machine continued to reject her because of the oversized belt buckle. Having been told by the attendants that she must take it off, the young lady, as we would say down home, threw a tantrum.

In a foreign language accompanied by appropriate hand gestures and stomping feet, this spitfire furious Latina regaled all about her, especially her companion, who was, in an apologetic tone, trying to get her to remove the buckle.

After passing through the metal detector, I stepped out of line and set my bags down, deciding to stay until the show was over. As I said, I'm easily entertained.

For a moment, it looked as if I had wasted my time, for suddenly the spitfire became very quiet, loosened her belt, and laid it on the conveyor, much to the relief of her companion.

She then reached up, starting at the top and began unbuttoning her blouse. She was three buttons down before her husband, or boyfriend, realized that she aimed to discard her shirt as well as her belt. He quickly reached up and began re-buttoning her blouse, all the while talking to her in a pleading tone. She proceeded all the way to the bottom of the shirt with the nimble-fingered young man never more than three button holes behind.

Having finished, she whirled away from her companion, stalked through the metal detector and with her nose high in the air, headed across the lobby toward a flight to Los Angeles. As the young man staggered away under the load of all their combined bags, purse, belt and jewelry, it dawned on me that the security crew at the metal detector had gone on with their business through this whole episode, as if nothing unusual had occurred.

I wonder what it would take to impress these people?

It often seems that human beings change in direct proportion to their density, much as white mice do in laboratory crowding experiments. Even after the flight attendant's careful explanation of the boarding sequence, one through twenty first, twenty through forty second, and so on, still the higher numbered passengers crowd to the front, clog the entrance to the loading ramp, and slow the boarding of the 747 Peoples Express jet that is to carry us to London.

Hanging back, doing as I am told, I smile smugly to myself as I watch others push and jostle their way to the front. Then I begin to wonder, could I be right, and all these more experienced travelers be wrong? Do they know something that I don't know? Could it possibly be first come first serve? Feeling a touch of panic, I edged into the crowd, my smugness having vanished. Another white mouse joins the mob.

After we are all aboard and settled into our seats, one passenger with a confirmed ticket is left wandering the aisle, searching for a seat, "stuck out" as we used to say. The stewardess, in a friendly voice, calls out the name of one of the standby passengers, asking him to report forward. No one moves.

In a little less pleasant voice, she spells out the name. Still, no one moves. This reminds me a lot of my mother calling me as a child when I would be playing down on the creek.

"Dean!" she would call. I would get real quiet.

"Dean Drew!" I would hold my breath. "Dean Drew Meeks!"

I always answered when she used all three names. I knew that she knew where I was. I also knew that she knew that I knew that she knew where I was! I never did find out which passenger got to ride and which had to deplane. I was just glad it wasn't me they were paging. If they called out all three of my names, I would just naturally give myself up.

~~~~

"My father was born in a log cabin, not far from where I am writing these words," Drew remembers. "He was born to a dairyman and his wife – Manson and Lois Meeks. Dean was the second son born to Manson and Lois, but later he was to have another brother brought into the home through a strange adoption.

"Lois was a nurse at the small Coryell County hospital and assisted in delivering babies. One child that she helped bring into the world lost his mother due to complications of childbirth in the 1940s. The father of the child took him home with the three other children he already had. A few days later, he returned to the hospital and gave my grandmother, Lois, the baby and asked if she could take him. The rancher could not raise the newborn and the other children without the help of his wife.

"Little is known to me about this other family. The story that my grandmother told me, when she was in her 90s, was that she brought the baby home and asked Manson if she could keep the child. He told her that they could not, but she kept him, anyway.

"My grandmother was sharing this story with me shortly before she died, and she was wondering if she had done the wrong thing by going against her husband. I told her that I didn't think she did anything wrong giving this child a good home. I felt that taking care of one of God's children was not an easy decision, but she did what was needed for the child. She told me what joy he brought to her. She took up photography, and he was the perfect little boy, sitting still for many of her photo sessions. The other two boys were older and helped on the dairy or ran the banks of Dodds Creek.

"Manson Meeks was a hard-working, fun loving, adventurous man. He was a gentle man, with a kind heart. He seemed to me to be fearless as he held a tarantula spider in his palm or picked up a

stinging scorpion by the tail. I remember him petting the back of a wild raccoon as the coon ate from the dairy cows' feed trough.

"Playing seemed to come just second to hard work for Manson. There were pulley swings from the old oak trees to the barn, and numerous floatation devices to run the treacherous waters of the Dodds Creek when it was rainy season (which were too few). I was about ten when Manson died suddenly, cleaning the lanes after the morning milking on a Saturday. He had a heart attack and was gone before I realized what a treasure he was.

"Dean, my dad, was raised in this loving home. Although he had an adventurous spirit, he was the one who continued to run the dairy and tend to his mother and his own family. By the time his dad died in 1972, Dean had married his one true love, Margaret Lynn Perryman, and they had two daughters."

~~~~

Dean's family log cabin (left to right) Dean, Lois, Manson, Weldon, Woody

What an interesting cross section of humanity I find aboard the Boeing 747 carrying me to England. The young lady sitting next to me is a student from New Jersey in her last year at Rutgers University. She is on her way to visit an uncle and four cousins, whom she has never seen, at her grandfather's farm in Ireland. Two seats forward, a group of Jewish people in high spirits are laughing and cutting up as they attempt – not very successfully – to cram a tremendous amount of carry-on luggage into the small overhead compartments. The men dressed in dark ethnic clothing, have shaved heads, long curled sideburns and wear black skull caps. The women and children are dressed typically American. Two of the older bearded grandfathers wear short sleeved shirts and boldly display symbols that were once a cause of shame.

A-46240 tattooed on the forearm of a big shambling man nearest me identifies him as a former inmate of the infamous WWII camps such as Dachau, Auschwitz, or Bergen-Belsen. What stories of hardship, horror, and endurance they could tell. I would love to talk with them, but they are speaking either German or Hebrew and seem well content with their own company right now.

Seated behind me are two punk rockers. The girl has shaved her head around the sides, leaving the top part of her hair sticking straight up, dyed green, orange, and black. Possibly the green is her natural hair color. She also left an orange pony tail down the back of her neck and has bat wings and spider webs painted on her cheeks. The boy, who has shaved and polished his head, wears brogan shoes and an over-sized checkered clown suit. Just your everyday, average couple.

Traveling from west to east, with the rotation of the earth, shortened the night to about four hours, and I'm sure I lost some sleep aboard that jet liner that I will never recover. As the big plane broke through the layered clouds on our descent to Gatwick airport, just south of London, I saw the beautiful English country side for the second time.

Some thirty years earlier returning from a three-year tour of duty with the paratroops in southern Germany, our troopship, the USS Brucker, had tied up alongside a dock in the south of England.

Although the fog was so thick you could have picked it like cotton standing at the ship rail, I could just make out the glow surrounding a street light and the faint edge of a stone pier some twenty yards away.

After this faint brush with England, the British Isles were added to the list of foreign countries visited in my travels, and I would easily be persuaded to talk at some length of the beauty and history of these misty isles!

Dean and Drew in London, England 1985

Chapter Six

At the Gatwick air terminal, I was taken in tow by my daughter and son-in-law, Drew and Marshal Brooks. While Drew and I talked, Marshal drove us north around London in their little Yugoslav car, always on the wrong side of the road. This turned out all right, for everyone else was driving on the wrong side, also.

Thinking that this left-hand rule would not affect me, as I would not be doing any driving, I later learned, nearly to my sorrow, that pedestrians also have a lot to lose if they look the wrong way for traffic as they cross a street.

The farmhouse where the kids lived was located several miles north of a quaint little stone village called Islesham. Built upon a small knoll and surrounded by flat fertile farmlands, this village was once an island in a broad tide wash and only accessible by land at low tide. The land, having been reclaimed from the cold North Sea by an extensive series of dikes, was now used mainly for growing vegetables and small grains. As I did a lot of walking along the back roads of these fens, it became apparent that an experienced hobo could live quite well by gleaning the assorted vegetables lost along the roadside. Potatoes, onions, carrots, and beets were plentiful, and if one should poach a partridge or a pheasant from the Queen's vast gentle flock, he could very easily build himself a nice roadside stew.

Using the Brooks' cottage as my home base, I began making exploratory trips to fishing villages and marinas along the southeastern English coast, from King's Lynn in the north to Portsmouth, south of London. The transit system in Britain is very old, reliable, and affordable, with buses and trains serving even the smallest towns, with, of course, the exception of Islesham.

As Drew and Marshal were always at work well before daylight, doing whatever airmen do, my trips would usually start with a four- to six-mile hike to some larger town where the buses ran regularly. Then, across the country in a bright red, double-decked bus to hit a train terminal at Ely, Cambridge, or Bury St. Edmunds. I like the buses and loved the trains.

29

Once on a return trip from the coast, I was waiting at a bus stop in New Market for a ride to Isleham. No buses showed up at the scheduled time, and I had about given up on it when I was joined by a young lady going the same direction. She questioned me as to whether the bus had already passed, and I assured her it hadn't, and it probably wouldn't, for it was quite a bit overdue and the last bus that evening. After explaining to me that by not having a bus at this stop at the proper time, the company was derelict in their duty to the public, she walked off towards the main station to see what they were going to do about it.

"A fat lot of good that will do," I thought to myself, throwing my light duffel bag over my shoulder and heading for the main highway north to try my luck at hitchhiking. I wasn't more than ten or fifteen miles from 'home,' but this could be a very long walk.

I hadn't been on the main road for more than fifteen minutes when what should appear but a bright red, double-decked bus that slowed to a stop and opened its doors to pick me up. Sure enough, upon clambering aboard, I found my friend from the bus stop to be the only passenger and the manager of the station, a big friendly talkative fellow, already off-duty, to be the driver. We sat up next to the driver and enjoyed a nice chat as he drove the over-sized bus down the narrow twisting roads to Isleham, as if this were the most natural occurrence in the world. Somehow, I feel that it would have been handled differently in the United States.

Another time, while walking at about the same place with my sea bag over my shoulder and my thumb stuck out, I got a ride with a big, tough-looking fella in a Mercedes, headed down to London.

He talked steadily as we sped down the roadway, every now and then glancing at me as if he expected a reply. I knew he was speaking the Cockney English of East London, but for the life of me, I could only catch a word now and then, and could make no sense of it at all.

When I finally spoke up and asked him to talk a little slower so that I could understand him, he jumped back startled and exclaimed, "Blimey, you're a bloody Yank."

Having very seldom been referred to as a Yank, I explained to him who I was, where I was from, and what I was doing, wandering around this beautiful countryside. He didn't seem too impressed with who I was or what I was doing over here. He only looked at me again and exclaimed in wonder, "I didn't know Yanks walked!"

There is probably no place in England, given the proper wind conditions and a little imagination, that you can't smell the sea. Nowhere that you can be more than a hundred miles from it. For a person that loves boats and history as I do, the coast of this island nation is a candy store where something new or half-forgotten is discovered in each cove, anchorage, or inlet. From the largest ocean-going oil tanker to the smallest oar-driven rowboat, every type of work or pleasure craft can be found venturing out to sea for pleasure or profit. Fishing boats, barges, coasters, ferries, sailboats, warships, tugboats, and ocean liners can be observed plying the toll-free superhighway that surrounds this maritime nation.

Often in search for the proper vessel to carry me back home, I would become sidetracked and find myself down at the fishing docks, watching as weary fisherman unloaded their night's catch, or alongside a cargo ship stacking itself with containerized cargo until it seemed it would capsize, or on a little muddy creek off the Orwell River where the pilgrims first set sail for the Americas, only to be forced into Plymouth by seasickness and bad weather, thus changing history. I suppose Plymouth Rock does sound better than Ipswitch Rock.

The vessel I was trying to locate had to be large enough to withstand the heavy seas and violent weather of an Atlantic crossing, yet small enough to fit into my gradually shrinking bank roll. Of the vast numbers of boats available for purchase, only a very few fit into this narrow category, and then usually one flaw or another eliminated them from consideration.

Although they were nowhere close to what I could afford, I was unable to resist checking out some of the fifty- or sixty-foot motor sail yachts that turned my head and made my mouth water, always assuring the owners that I would probably get back in touch with them after considering all of the possibilities – or rob Fort Knox!

Finally, in an out-of-the-way marina, a wet three-mile walk from a country bus stop, I located the boat that seemed to fit all my needs and my pocketbook.

The White Swan, a thirty-foot sloop, white with blue trim, rode the slight swells at her birth with easy grace, sitting a little heavy in the water and showing no wasted motion. She was built for cruising, not racing, having a large mahogany planked cabin that was six feet from deck to overhead, making it easy to get about in for most people. Unfortunately, I am six feet two inches. At times, however, this gave one more point to wedge against when the seas were up, and things got rowdy inside.

She was well set up, having a sturdy aluminum mast well-braced by heavy steel cables that were doubled aft and tripled forward. Six more of these heavy stays, three to port and three to starboard, gave me the impression the mast would be there come hell or high water.

Mounted in a cradle on the bow, easily accessible, was a heavy Danforth anchor, its long, galvanized chain leading down a house hole to a chain locker directly below. In a stern locker, another anchor, slightly lighter, was located along with several hundred feet of heavy nylon line.

The engine, a gasoline powered affair built in the Netherlands, and having a mind of its own, was recessed into the aft section of the cabin and could be reached for maintenance and repair from the cockpit or the cabin. Later, after I had finalized the purchase, several marina hands, who had hardly spoken earlier and had offered no advice or help at all, were aghast and very vocal about the fact that I had purchased a vessel with gasoline power rather than diesel. Apparently, gasoline is considered very dangerous aboard a vessel at sea because of the fire hazard and there being no place to run in an emergency. But, for me, this was the right choice as I knew very little about gasoline engines and absolutely nothing at all about diesels!

The cabin was beautiful. Although the hull of the Swan was made of tough fiberglass, most of the interior was filled out with a dark, heavy-grained wood that I took to be mahogany. Two full-size bunks were located along either side of the main cabin, above which were double banks sturdy lockers.

Aft of the port side bunk was the galley, consisting of a cook stove, sink, and pantry. The stove, mounted upon gimbals, swung free and remained nearly level no matter what tune the sea had the Swan dancing to. Thus, the crew, even in bad weather, had access to hot food and coffee whether their stomachs were up to it or not.

Aft the other bunk, placed so the stairway served as a stool, was a desk and chart table above which was mounted an instrument panel for the engine, electrical systems, and ship to shore radio. Forward the main cabin was the lavatory, a nice convenient facility to use while tied up in a calm marina; a carnival crazy house on a dark and stormy night at sea. Forward the lavatory was another small cabin containing two bunks and doubling as a sail locker. Here I discovered a large jumble of bags crammed full of sails of every size and description, some of which I recognized and some of which I didn't.

The owner and his family had the Swan well-stocked with all the little odds and ends that would be needed to deal with minor emergencies and add comfort to a long voyage. They agreed to leave most of this aboard, for it would be impossible for me to replace this collection in a short period of time, when they had spent over a decade putting together.

The whole family was eager to help me master all the little quirks and eccentricities to be encountered aboard their floating home away from home. The longer we talked, the more they discovered how little I knew, so the more they taught.

Their son, perhaps twelve years old, carried me from stern to stern, explaining the plumbing and electrical systems. While his folks and older sister cleared their personal belongings from the lockers, this young Lord Nelson sailor gave me a crash course on the use of the navigational equipment aboard.

As we closed the deal on the Swan, I offered the family fifty pounds extra if they would throw in the boy as a first mate. Although his sister thought this was more than he was worth and liked the idea, his parents assured me they already had quite a large investment in him and probably, since he had a ferocious appetite, I couldn't afford to feed him anyway.

Chapter Seven

On the Orwell

What seemed like a relatively easy voyage, studied by a warm fireplace on rainy afternoons in Coryell County, becomes much more complicated as I go along.

I seem to remember the English Channel being light blue, calm, and sunny on the National Geographic maps at home. Over here on the local charts, I am surprised to find that it is filled with sand bars, mud flats, wrecked ships, the heaviest sea traffic in the world, and the nastiest weather you can imagine.

Of course, there were no tides on Lake Belton, and the Gulf of Mexico only rose and fell a couple of feet, noticeable only to the practiced eye. Here, on the eastern coast of England, to be ignorant of the tides could be dangerous, if not fatal. Luckily, I received my education in small doses that didn't choke me too much.

One sunny afternoon, Drew and Marshal showed up with their little car packed full of canned and dried goods to stock the lockers of the White Swan. After the last can of soup was aboard, we put out into the Orwell estuary to see how we would stack up against the other weekend sailors cruising or racing up and down this inland waterway in their brightly-painted craft.

I had been out twice alone on the Swan, and in this narrow body of water, the frequency of changing tack when going to windward had taken all the pleasure out of the cruise. Now, with a couple of quick, strong deckhands aboard – though neither had sailed before – we soon had the Swan dancing to our tune, so that none of the Limey's sailing alongside suspected she had three Texas cowboys for a crew.

After sailing for about an hour in the bay, we pulled down the sails and proceeded up the river under power to look at the hundreds of boats either anchored in the channel or tied up along the shore.

A group of eight or ten ancient black wooden sailing barges, lined up along the bank, held my attention as we cruised nonchalantly up the river. Marshal had just gone forward to watch for obstructions when Drew called out from the cabin, asking whether the depth finder was working properly, as it was pegged out on zero.

I had paid no attention at all to the depth finder, for we were about fifty yards out from these large Thames barges that seemed to be sitting deep into the water. Quickly cutting the power and slipping the gears to neutral, I felt the sickening tug on the keel and the rapid deceleration that said very plainly we were aground.

Hoping to be lucky and ease her stern first back into deeper water, I moved the gears to reverse and slowly increased power. Tremendous amounts of black mud and water boiled up astern the Swan, but no movement could be detected. Marshal, in the meantime, had broken out the spinnaker boom and was trying to pole from the bow, only to have the boom swallowed up in the bottomless black ooze.

The tide, which I had ignored before now, became very important in this situation. If it were rising, we could simply wait until we were buoyed up out of the mud and set free. One look over the side at the water flowing seaward told me that just the opposite was true. The tide was falling, and if we fail to get off this mud bar quickly, it would be about twelve hours before we would get another chance.

Leaving Drew to operate the engine and Marshal to pole from forward, I took off shoes and shirt and dropped over the side into the coldest water I can ever remember being in. The cold water completely took my breath away and paralyzed my body until a welcome numbness took over, allowing me to get short jerky breaths of air, as I waded neck-deep around the prow of the mired Swan.

Marshal, who abandoned the spinnaker boom as useless, quickly joined me, and together we tried to push the boat astern, while Drew revved the engine in reverse. All we managed to do was push ourselves down into the cold, bottomless mud.

Looking at my son-in-law, who was blonde-haired and very light-complexioned, I was forced to laugh, even in our discomfort. Marshal had actually turned blue! Through chattering teeth, he informed me that I looked no better as we dragged our numbed bodies back aboard the Swan. To me, this looked like a good place to spend the night.

This section of the eastern coast of England has about a twelve-foot tide, and we had gone aground near its crest. In half an hour, our beautiful craft lay on her side at a forty-nine-degree angle in the black, slimy, ancient mud of the river Orwell.

Having read that the inn at Pin Mill was a good place to eat, we decided to slither across the mud flats and have supper there. Drew, being the lightest, was elected (two to one) to be the guinea pig and test the depth of the muck. After watching her sink nearly to her knees in the slime, Marshal and I rolled our britches legs very high, tied our shoes around our necks and followed Drew as she struggled toward the dry land. Above the sucking sound of feet being pulled from the goo, Drew was heard to ask, "Are we still having fun?"

Pin Mill, now a nice pub and restaurant, once produced most of the belaying pins used in the British Navy. These hardwood pins, about the size of a policeman's billy club, and often used as one, were located along the rails of sailing ships and used to tie off ropes quickly by looping a series of figure eights about them.

As we ate our seafood and chips, we could see the White Swan out in the mud flats far from any water, laying on her side at a very ungraceful angle. In all probabilities, earlier diners had recently been entertained by watching our unsuccessful efforts to re-float the Swan. In fact, I took some comfort in knowing that this little show had probably been repeated at intervals back through the ages to when man first began using boats as transportation. Possibly Hadrian's Roman troops aboard their invading ships had mired in this very spot, as the wild Britains' laughing and hooting shook their spears at them and jeered from the shore.

As we walked along the shore on our return to the Swan, we spent some time examining the huge black barges that had lured us into this inlet in the first place. They had not been afloat as I had presumed when I first saw them, rather being permanently impounded in the soft river bottom and having only a few inches of water lapping against their sides at high tide. Also, to our surprise, they were not abandoned hulks, but were rather ingeniously being used as dwellings, one being fixed up as a disco or perhaps a hippy's pad.

Needing to borrow a wrench to replace a broken generator belt on the Swan, we used this as an excuse to clamber up the rickety catwalks and examine more closely these converted coal and grain carriers. The cluttered derelict appearance of the exteriors gave no clue to the pleasant comfortably furnished interiors to be found aboard these old barges. Water lines and electricity came aboard from the shore, and the yard never needed mowing.

A gentleman aboard one of these barges had the wrench we needed and was glad to loan it to the Yanks that were aground in his back pasture. After much scraping and washing to get the tar-like mud off their legs, the kids went aboard to work on the generator, while I set about to make sure we pulled free of this mud bank at the next high tide.

Remembering some of the yachting technique I had acquired in the Gatesville library, I broke out the Swan's second anchor and maybe a hundred feet of heavy nylon line. Attaching one end of the line to a cleat, I carried the anchor as far astern as the line would allow, burying it securely in the mud. This should allow us to winch the Swan backward off the mud flat in case the high tide didn't raise the vessel clear of the bottom.

As the tide would not crest again until four thirty-three the next morning, we set about fixing up some makeshift bunks, the angle at which the Swan lay making it impossible to use the regular ones. The kids bunked down on the cabin bulkhead, while I made me a nest in the sail bags up forward. We were a long time getting to sleep, for each time it became quiet someone came up with a humorous comment that kept others giggling like school girls.

My memory isn't as good as it used to be, and if someone should ask me what I did Wednesday a week ago, I would be hard-pressed to tell them. I assured both Drew and Marshal, though, that this was one night they would remember very well for the rest of their lives.

Swan on her side~Orwell River

~~~~

"There we were," Drew says, "on the river Orwell. It was a cool morning, and I'm sure there was some fog. As I remember, all mornings were cool and foggy.

"I actually think it was my first-ever ride on a sailboat since dad took up sailing after I was off his payroll. Now, mind you, in my eyes, my dad could do anything. It never occurred to me to be worried or afraid about anything when dad was around.

"As I read over his journals, I realize how blessed I was that I ever saw him again. Anyway, there we were, having a grand time sailing up the river and enjoying the sites of the British countryside. I was checking out dad's new boat when I noticed that the depth finder was "stuck" on ZERO! Not thinking we were aground, I just *mentioned to dad that it must be broken or something, because it was on zero. Many a ranch truck speedometer did not work, so it was no big deal ... or was it?*

"Dad seemed to think it was a very big deal, and our leisurely sail quickly turned to a not-so-leisurely attempt to stop the forward progress of the boat. We finally decided – or the tides decided – that that was the place we would stay until morning.

"When dad wrote that we sailed triumphantly back to our berth at the marina, he left out one little detail. Or maybe after the long, cold night, he did not want to mention one more misadventure.

"As Marshal recalls, when the boat was righted, and we were backing out, one of the anchor lines became entangled in the propeller. My dad, who rarely said a cuss word, found a few that morning, as he had to go back overboard and untangle the rope from the propeller.

"I know that I was cold all night and I can't imagine how cold it was in that water at five in the morning. But untangle the rope he did, and then we sailed or limped back to the marina.

"I believe that was the last time I saw him before his voyage. I'm sure my goodbye was quick, as all I wanted to do was get warm – which I found to be very difficult in the dampness of England. You really can't appreciate the dry Texas heat until you stay wet and cold for a period of time."

~~~~

In the damp darkness of the Swan's interior, we needed no alarm clock to tell us that the tide was nearing its crest. As the Swan righted herself and came back to an even keel, we were tumbled out of our beds onto the deck, cold and sleepy. Up above in the biting rain with Marshal poling, Drew at the engine controls, and I winching in on the anchor line, we slowly dragged the Swan clear of the clinging mud and back to a navigable depth. In a pouring rain, under sail, wet, cold, and muddy, at five thirty in the morning, we sailed triumphantly back to our berth at the Marina.

40

I think the reason so many Englishmen go to sea is that it is the only way they can stay warm and dry. In this country of perpetual bad weather, the clouds come across in lines like marching soldiers, thirty minutes of sunshine, fifteen minutes of rain. And it's cold!

In the middle of June, your breath makes steam.

Yesterday was Margaret's birthday. The kids and I tried several times to call her but could not get through. When we finally completed the call, no one was home. I hope she's out having a party!

Tomorrow morning, if the weather stays bad but doesn't get worse, I intend to sail out of this Marina and head for home. I am not ready, still having a long list of things that must be done or supplies that are not yet aboard. Somehow the list of things needed continually gets longer instead of shorter, so I have decided to just cast off and go. Maybe I should use the rule of thumb said to be used in British naval shipyards: when the weight of the paperwork is equal to the weight of the water displaced by the ship, it is ready to be launched.

I have managed to get my one crew member aboard and operating in a satisfactory manner. This little electronic sailor, a Navico Auto Tiller which I promptly dubbed NAT, will hopefully mind the tiller and hold the Swan on the designated compass heading, freeing me to mind the sails and possibly get a little sleep every now and then. NAT is electrically operated off of the ship's batteries and works similar to a good right arm, either pushing or pulling the tiller to keep the vessel on course, paying little attention to the cold and rain.

Taking advantage of the plentiful fresh water here at the Marina, I have washed all my dirty clothes and hung them out to dry all about the Swan. Three or four times they were nearly dry, only to be re-rinsed by the showers to come across at regular intervals. I'm sure my neighboring yachtsmen will be glad to be rid of me, for I seem to be the only one with laundry draped about.

Chapter Eight

Well before daylight, I slipped my lines and moved out into the Orwell estuary. One lone gull, sitting under a light on a pylon at the end of the breakwater and reminding me of Edgar Allen Poe's Raven, followed my progress with a steady gaze as I moved the Swan through the marina entrance.

Tower Bridge-London. Talking to the "Raven"

Bucking both tide and headwind, I continued down the estuary under power, not choosing to break out the sails until I had cleared Felixstowe and gained the North Sea. The weather had improved very little, the temperamental wind coming in gusts from the North East with patches of dense fog separated by patches of not-so-dense fog.

As NAT was still below in a box, getting the sails up without losing control of the boat was difficult, to say the least. It consisted of tying off the tiller, sprinting forward on the slippery deck, hoisting and tying off a sail, then getting back to the cockpit before the Swan wandered off on a course of her own or came about into the wind!

I could see right away that NAT's strong right arm was going to be indispensable, as often aboard a sailing vessel this size, there are just too many jobs that demand immediate attention. On this first day of the long voyage, it seemed that I was either doing everything wrong or at least the hard way, finding myself give out and frustrated by noon.

Things became easier after the NAVICO Auto Tiller was installed and took over the helm, freeing me to munch on a can of cold beans. I immediately noticed that NAT had a much steadier hand on the tiller than I had, was less easily distracted by other shipping, and pushed on through thick fog banks with practically no deviation from the course dialed into his compass.

The thing most intolerable to both NAT and me were the calms – sometimes lasting half an hour – that beset the Swan off and on throughout the day. NAT would have to be disengaged to keep it from constantly jerking the rudder back and forth in a vain attempt to hold a course when the boat wasn't going anywhere. The White Swan, so graceful and sturdy in a strong breeze, became in a calm as disoriented as a country kid at his first dance. Knocked about by a short choppy sea that sent the boom careening back and forth across the cockpit, she wallowed and rolled helplessly, circling first one way and then another.

Having decided to stick to sailing as much as possible and not start the engine every time the wind died, I spent my time eating crackers to ward off seasickness and watching out for the heavy sea traffic in this area.

I was in what was probably the biggest shipping lane on Earth, for all the ships plying the coast of Europe are funneled through this narrow strip of water between England and France. There were Soviet ships loaded to the waterline with lumber, Japanese ships stacked precariously high with cargo containers, Greek oil tankers, and many others whose flags I did not recognize.

Although I was trying hard to keep a close eye out for any vessels on a collision course with the Swan, a large tanker slipped up on us from directly astern nearly blasting us out of the water with his fog horn. I'll bet the bridge watch had a good laugh as I almost jumped overboard. Being the overtaken vessel, I knew that by maritime law, I had the right-of-way and could hold my course if I so desired. Given the difference in the size of the two vessels and the possibility that they might not have even seen me, I quickly took the tiller from NAT and with a 90° turn to starboard, I gave them the sea lane.

The erratic winds, usually from directly astern, were also a reason for concern, as quite often a heavy roll by the Swan and a slight shift in wind direction would cause a jib by the mainsail boom. The wind, shifting to the backside of the sail, would send the heavy metal boom whistling across the cockpit about head high, taking with it over the side anything that was in its path. One glancing blow right at the top of the head taught me to avoid the boom as if it were a Texas diamondback rattlesnake.

As I worked about the boat, I learned to listen to the sails, as they would usually warn me of something amiss. As long as the mainsail made a humming sound, things were okay, but let it get quiet, followed by a rustling of canvas, then look out, the boom was coming across.

Along about mid-afternoon, with NAT at the helm and a steady wind from astern, I decided it was time to start enjoying this voyage. As the rain had stopped, and the sun was trying to break through the thinning fog, I stretched myself out on the cushioned bench in the cockpit and started to reread Michener's, "Tales of the South Pacific," one of my favorites.

I must've dozed off, as I was startled awake by hail from a passing trawler. The trawler captain, using a megaphone, warned me that I was approaching shallow water and if I didn't "alter to the North," I would soon be aground. Shouting my thanks to the fisherman and bringing the Swan quickly around to the recommended heading, I was just able to make out breakers, some two hundred yards off the port side.

Something was very wrong, for according to my calculations, I should be in deep water, about mid-channel between Dover and Calais, France.

As the evening wore on and the fog thickened, I began encountering shallows in any direction I chose to sail, groping about between the bars and becoming completely frustrated. Finally, as darkness set in about me, I pull down the sails and in the lee of a sandbar, dropped anchor for the night – tired, frustrated, and cold. Forgoing supper, I clawed my way out of my rain gear and into a warm bunk, thanking the Lord that although I was hopelessly lost, I was still afloat.

(June 14, 1985)

Come daylight, with a good breakfast of bacon, toast, and coffee under my belt, it was back on deck with an improved attitude, ready to do battle with whatever the day would bring.

I hoped for a clear day, for I needed some landmark to pinpoint my location, having no idea at all where I had anchored last night. On deck, I was once again greeted with the same fog and drizzle of yesterday, seemingly the standard fare for this part of the world.

After wrestling the anchor out of the deep mud and into its hangar on the bow of the Swan, I cranked the engine and headed the boat into the wind to ease the task of setting the sails. Turning the tiller over to NAT, I set the jib and was hauling up the mainsail when, with a loud thump, the deck was knocked from under my feet. Landing flat on my back on the narrow strip of the deck between the cabin and the port side rail, I quickly rolled to my knees to see with what we had collided, fearing the worst.

A large, round metal buoy about half the size of the Swan, grated along the starboard side of my craft, broke free near stern, and disappeared into the fog from which it had come. Luckily, it was only a glancing blow, and though I could find no damage above the waterline, I kept glancing into the cabin the rest of the day, hoping not to see my gear afloat!

After meandering in a westerly direction for about an hour, I came upon three large freighters anchored in a line, each about a mile

45

apart. I sailed slowly by each in turn, yelling and trying to attract attention, hoping to get someone aboard to give me our location. I saw no life at all on any of the ships, not even getting a bark from the ship's dog.

A little further west, I made landfall, and upon locating a little old lady out on a pier, was informed after much shouting back and forth that I was just off Southend-on-Sea. This couldn't be possible! I knew I was no "Henry the Navigator," but I could hardly believe I was this far off course so early into my voyage. Had I continued much further west I would've sailed right up the Thames into downtown London.

As I sailed back East along the Kentish shore, I pondered my situation, finally coming to some conclusions that were later confirmed by sailors more experienced with these waters than me. Upon sailing into the narrows at the eastern end of the English Channel, I had unknowingly been bucking a very strong tide which had about halved to my southern progress. Also, as this mass of water swept east to refill the Thames estuary, it had carried the Swan several miles off our course and into the shallows that dot these roads.

A little after noon, upon setting a new course south into the straights of Dover, I was confronted by the infamous Goodwin Sands, a dangerous line of shoals that have come to be known as "the ship swallower." These Sands over the centuries have devoured countless ships.

Once, in 1703, a sudden gale wrecked thirteen ships of the British fleet, with the loss of twelve hundred men. Two American ships, lost in 1946, can be seen when the tide is low, and other older wrecks are said to be exposed by the sands for short periods of time, then reburied, as if the sands were showing off their catch. You can bet that I, NAT, and the Swan tiptoed through that boiling water with eyes as big as saucers, like kids going through a graveyard at midnight on Halloween night.

The weather was much improved, the sun clearing away the fog and making the beautiful white cliffs around Dover look like something on a picture postcard. Brightly colored lighthouses spaced along the green top cliffs soon raised my spirits and had me singing salty sea ditties as I worked about the Swan, drying out from the miserable weather we had just come through. With cousin Ranzell's Swiss Army knife and some safety wire put aboard by the kids, I rebuilt the brackets that held the Navico Auto Tiller to the gunwale, these having been torn loose when we collided with the buoy this morning.

~~~~

"On November 26, 2008, cousin Ranzell gifted me with the Swiss Army knife that daddy carried on his trip," Drew says. "This is a little history of the knife in Ranzell's words ..."

"'January 1984, this knife was given to me by a German woman named Irene (Joe Ambrose's girlfriend). She flew the knife from Germany to Killeen. Then, before Dean left for his trip, I sent it with him and asked that, if possible, he would return it to me. Dean Meeks flew it from Houston to England and carried it about 2,900 miles on a sailboat from England to France-Spain-Portugal-Morocco-North Africa, then to the Canary Islands and then Senegal, west side of Africa. Then, flew to Houston and back to Meeks Dairy-ville-on Dodds Creek at Gatesville, Texas, and returned it to me on the 12th day of September 1985.'

~~~~

In the afternoon, my progress along the southern English coast came to a standstill as the spanking breeze that had carried us along died to nothing, leaving the water completely calm. Taking advantage of the calm, I stripped off my clothes, intending to go over the side into the dark green water for a much-needed bath. I changed my mind and decided to use a bucket and washcloth, as something

47

big and black swam beneath the boat, and I didn't even want to know what it was!

My sailing cap, given to me by my friend, C. F., back in Houston, was flipped off my head by a loose line and lost overboard before we even cleared the Orwell River. I'm now down to an old cowboy hat that, with the brim turned down all around and a three-day growth of beard, makes me look like Indiana Jones – well, maybe Yasser Arafat.

Giving up on the wind, I anchored the Swan in some shaley rocks beneath the cliffs east of Folkstone, got out my copy of Reed's National Almanac, and used the last hour of daylight to improve my sailing skills. The previous owners, having left the almanac aboard for my use, told me it contained all the nautical information that I would ever need to know.

As the sun dipped itself into the Atlantic far to the west, I was on page twelve with only thirteen hundred and one pages to go.

1985   Selfie

Chapter Nine

I have never read anything about the man or woman that invented the hammock, or the adoption of their creation to ocean-going vessels, but the two creations were bound to come together as sure as peaches and cream.

I didn't have a hammock to neutralize the role and pitch of the Swan last night as she tethered in this choppy sea, but I did have a folding sideboard on my bunk that at least kept my body from spilling over onto the deck. I suppose it would be similar to sleeping in a very narrow casket with the lid open, although I'd rather not dwell long on that supposition.

When the weather is fair as it is today, the cliffs along the southeastern coast of England are startlingly beautiful. Dark water, bright sky, gleaming white cliffs capped with a carpet of emerald green grass gives a feeling of freshness, as though the world was newly created, and you were breathing air never before inhaled by living beings.

This rich feeling quickly vanishes, though, as a speeding train roars from a hidden tunnel halfway up the cliff, releases a screaming challenge from its abrasive horn, then plunges its centipede like body back into the dark innards of the mountain. A roaring, screaming, rumbling, apparition that vanishes as quickly as it appeared, leaving me wondering if I really saw a train or was I perhaps as daft as some had hinted.

Here beneath the white cliffs of Folkstone and Dover, I began to learn about anchors and anchorages. On our small lake back home, you simply drop anchor over the side anywhere you please, with very little regard for conditions on the bottom. Here, I had anchored in a small niche whose bottom was strewn with large slabs of shale rock and boulders. The anchor held firmly during the long restless night and just as firmly when I tried to bring it back aboard the next morning.

Looping the galvanized chain around one shoulder and across my back, I gave it my best effort, using back and leg muscles. The anchor held firm, but my back gave way. It was several days before I could straighten up without the feeling that someone was probing around my backbone with an ice pick.

Being no longer able to use my back, I was forced to use my head and soon came up with the means of dislodging my reluctant anchor from its rocky hold.

Catching the bow at its lowest point between swells, I threw a couple of half-hitches of anchor chain around a cleat and made it fast. I felt sure that the weight of the boat rising with the next swell would furnish the pull and jerk needed to set us free to continue the voyage. Disappointment and foreboding began to set in, as swell after swell failed to yield any results. While muttering to myself and groping about in my almost empty bag of tricks, I noticed a very large swell moving toward the Swan from the east. A VERY LARGE SWELL! If the Swan didn't rise with this one, it looked as though we might be pulled under.

I jumped atop the cabin and held on to the mast as the bow and foredeck was pulled beneath the green flood. With a grinding wrench and shutter, the Swan broke free and bobbed to the surface, sloughing water off her decks and gasping for air, free at last!

As I brought up the chain, I was heartened to feel the weight of the anchor at its end, as I wasn't sure up until then whether the anchor had broken loose fair, or the chain had parted. Though I had thought it bad luck to lose my sailing cap over the side before clearing the Orwell River, it would have been much worse to have lost the Swan's main anchor while still in sight of the English coast.

White Cliffs of Dover

(Sunday, June 16, 1985 – Father's Day)

After two tedious days sailing along England's south coast, I have gained much experience and very little mileage. I am learning that the greatest problem of sailing single-handed is that you never have enough manpower when things really get sticky. Not wanting to endanger another person's life by my inexperience was a major consideration in my deciding to sail alone, along with the fact that I don't like being in charge of others or having others in charge of me.

Also, years ago, I had read a piece by an Antarctic explorer, possibly Admiral Byrd, about the stress placed on small groups of people isolated together over long periods of time. If such an undertaking could not consist of at least five people, he concluded, it would be best to go it alone, which he did, spending a winter by himself in the Antarctic near the South Pole.

51

Indifferent breezes and runaway tides have kept me hustling about the decks of the Swan in a seemingly futile attempt to make westerly progress into an easterly wind. At times, when the winds are slack, and the tide is surging happily back into the North Sea, I can – by marking my position on the shoreline – watch as my craft makes her way, stern first, back along the route we have just covered.

When the breezes strengthen, even though from directly ahead, I can make fair progress by getting up all the canvas I can safely handle. Being unfamiliar with the Swan and saltwater sailing, I was reluctant to put up more sail than I can get down quickly, in case of a sudden storm. By replacing the foresail with a working jib, I have added several knots to our progress and raised my spirits slightly above the deck. When conditions become more favorable, I have several large Genoas still bagged up in the sail locker that I intend to air out. I have never handled this type of sail before, but I am certain there is a half-page in Reed's nautical almanac that will adequately cover the subject.

Also below, folded neatly in the sail locker, is a storm jib, a small triangle of tough heavy canvas to be used as a foresail in really violent weather. With the storm jib set and the mainsail reefed down to handkerchief-size, you should be able to maintain steerage without danger of the craft being laid over on her side in a gale. When showing me this sail, Mr. Brown, the previous owner, was quick to mention that he had never had to use it.

To me, this sounded a little like someone back home, while trying to sell a well-worn saddle, casually mentioning that, "Yes, it has a saddle horn, but I've never had to grab it."

Day before yesterday, we made a passage through the infamous "Goodwin Sands" off Kent, just north of Dover. It is known as "the ship swallower," for it has devoured countless ships over the centuries.

I didn't know that the palm of your hand could sweat!

Yesterday was spent tacking back and forth into stiff headwinds, and after traveling a thousand miles, I gained thirty. Well, as my sweet mother-in-law used to say, "Every little bit added to a little bit makes it a little bit more." It is still very cold and bucking a ten-knot wind, plus the four-knot headway you are making, makes it seem like a gale.

While getting the anchor up out of the rocks yesterday, I messed up my back again, and my bum wrist is killing me from tugging on the tiller. I wonder if Doc Wilson makes house boat calls. This morning, when weighing anchor, I thought of my neighbor, Gene Chitwood, when he proposed to his wife, Diane.

He told her he had two questions: "Will you marry me?"

"Yes," was her reply.

Then she asked, "What was your second question?" To that he replied, "Will you help me get up off my knees?" I know the feeling.

Well, today, wind has slacked to near nothing, but the sun is out and it's good clothes-drying weather. My favorite shirt seems to have terminal ring around the collar, and my white socks, even after washing, look like my foster boys' socks used to look after three days camping out on the Dodds Creek.

No wind at all this morning, but I've got my kicker running, heading west a few miles off the coast at Eastbourne. If I pick up any kind of wind at all, I should be to the Isle of Wight by dark. HAL is at the helm, and I'm busy doing laundry and minor repairs. I don't worry about getting my laundry white any more – just a lighter shade of gray will do fine.

By the way, I have renamed my automatic tiller. He now answers to the name of HAL, after the reluctant and rebellious computer aboard the space probe in the book, "2001: A Space Odyssey." I noticed the similarity when I gave a command that was rather difficult, and although he did the job, he coughed and kind of cleared his throat as he did it!

Well, the heck with the British coast and the Isle of Wight and their contrary winds, I've struck out for France with a fair wind, though it is a bit southerly. I think HAL agrees as I caught just a flicker of a smile on his compass face when we changed course. He wanted to turn earlier, but I like being close to land.

HAL, formerly known as NAT.

Chapter Ten

(Monday, June 17, 1985)

Sailed all night last night, or most of it. I feel like I've been on a three-day trail ride. I've had my coffee cold, too weak, too strong, too sweet, every bad way you can have it, but the worst way you can have it is in your lap. Well, I guess I'm lucky, it could have been my oatmeal!

Along the southern coast of England, you could spend a long time visiting places where Romans, Normans, Vikings, and many others came ashore, fought, built fortifications, then were integrated into the British people. I love history and have enjoyed picking out these places and trying to reconstruct how it was.

But this morning, I'm sailing ten or twelve miles off a coast and a battlefield that is not history to me. I was nine or ten years old when the English, Americans, Free French, and many other allies stormed ashore on the beaches of Normandy to start the final push to rid Europe and the world of a cancerous growth called Nazi-ism. Dieppe, St. Martin, Omaha, and Utah beaches, all places where fathers and uncles of ours stepped up with clenched teeth and a tight smile and plunked down their lives to buy a little more freedom for the ones they loved.

Maybe we need to pat the survivors on the back one more time while they are still around.

No sun, no sky, no horizon, no wind, and the ocean is a dull gray and smooth as glass. No progress. What of the English, Spanish, and French fleets dashing about in the old days giving battle to one and all? Must have had better wind in those days. I guess I'd better enjoy the calm, though, because I'm sure there'll be days when I'll have much more wind than I'll have use for.

(June 18, 1985)

All my charts show the Doldrums to be in the mid-North Atlantic. Well, they have kin folks here in the Baie de la Seine, off the coast of France. A large French fishing trawler came roaring by this morning. The skipper came out on deck, made motions as if he were blowing some wind in my limp sails, then grinned and waved. I weakly grinned back, waved, and muttered, "Not funny, Pierre."

(June 19 and 20, 1985)

Spent several hours trying to round Cape Barfleur, just east of Cherbourg, France. Finally gave up and found a somewhat calm spot to wait for the tide to change, and all the water to run the other way, and run it does.

High tide was at midnight, but I missed it by about an hour. I had a fair wind and the tide was in the right direction, but as I came around the Cape, about three miles out in the pitch dark, I begin to hear a roar that sounded like the Cow House Creek on a big rise. All I could figure was breakers on rocks, but there were no rocks here on my charts.

I tried to alter course and pull away, but we were being drawn in faster than I could sail away. With my light, I picked up what was making the roar. Ahead was a four-foot wall of water, breaking like a wave on the beach but staying in one place, with the calmer water that I was in racing into it. I didn't have any choices, so I turned into it, held on tight and muttered the battle cry of the Gatesville Olympic ski team, "Are we still having fun?"

Once into what I later learned was a riptide, old Swan spun, bucked, and jumped like a bronc but otherwise there was no damage, unless it was to my underwear. I went through three more of those that night, all just like the first. The next day was rough, but that's another story as I'm trying to get this in the mail.

I'm in St. Peter's Port on the Isle of Guernsey getting water, gas, and food at my last English-speaking port for a while. In fact, this is the first time in seven days that I have set foot on land. It feels just exactly like trying to walk normal after roller skating. And wouldn't you know, I got land sick.

Please save these papers for me. Dean

(Port St. Peter – June 21, 1985)

Days like today are the rewards for all the hard time you spend getting to them. Who said cowboys can't get lucky some of the time!

This morning, rain and squalls out of the South (gale force 8, whatever that means) kept me in port again. In port, you can pick and choose your weather, a luxury not permitted at sea, so this morning I toured the island on the local buses and stayed away from the expensive tour bus service, making the complete circuit for a little over a dollar.

I did a lot of walking, which I like, and got very wet, which I don't like. The country is very beautiful, but much too crowded for a person from Central Texas.

Their largest export – I presume going to England – are fresh-cut flowers. There are thousands of green houses, and as you walk down the very narrow rock-walled roads, each house has a display of flowers and vegetables where you can shop on the honor system, take what you want and drop the money in the box. A dozen roses for thirty cents and a dozen tomatoes for the same price, and they'll nearly give you the potatoes!

The cattle I saw, naturally, were all Guernsey, and being an old dairy hand, I could appreciate their fine quality. I've seen a lot of older pictures around of the smiling farmer holding his prize-winning cow by the halter, while his not-so-smiling wife does the milking. But like I say, they were older pictures.

This island was occupied by the German Army during World War II and liberated by the U.S. Army in May of 1945. A large L.S.T. (Landing Ship, Tank) pulled into the harbor at high water and when the tide went out, left her high and dry. Then they simply drove ashore with food and supplies for the people of the island. There was no fighting, for the Germans were waiting to surrender. Needless to say, we are still well-thought of here, even after forty years.

But here's the high point of my day. There is an old square-rigged sailing ship back in one of the repair docks, being fitted out to carry working passengers on cruises all around Europe. I hung around taking pictures until I was invited aboard by a young lady who turned out to be the First Mate. Her mate was high in the rigging doing some cable repair. I was allowed to wander around on deck and down below in all the clutter that goes with sailing ships. I was in, as they say, Hog Heaven!

When Tim came down out of the rigging, I was invited into the galley for coffee, with a little rum in it, and as it was so rainy and cold, I couldn't refuse. Several other crew members came in, and when they learned of my undertaking, they spent the next hour giving me a cram course in coastal navigation and any information they thought would help on my trip. I naturally adopted them all as fellow Texans, for they were my kind of people.

Then, it really got good.

I asked for, and received, permission to go aloft up the mainmast, ninety feet above deck, something I've always wanted to do, but never really expected. The ship was pitching, and it was raining steadily. I was whipped around up there like the last kid in line playing "pop the whip."

I had about the same feeling as I did when I put the last rocking chair on the ball of the water tower on Tenth Street one Halloween night back in the '50s.

It's impossible for me to imagine how a person would have the nerve to go aloft and furl the top gallant in pitch dark, during a violent storm, with everything whipping about, rain pouring down and the only light being from lightning, when the "devil blinked his eyes." It's near impossible to furl a sail on my sloop in high winds and heavy seas with both feet firmly (or not so firmly) on deck.

Sail in this Tall Ship!

No previous sailing experience needed.

The Schooner "Jacques Cartier"

Master: John Cluett

Length overall 110ft
Beam 21ft
Draft 10ft

Height of mast above water 85ft
Engine 360hp Diesel
Electricity: 220, 110, 24 volts DC

From her home port in Guernsey, this sturdy wood-built ship is now at your service for day trips, long weekends and voyages of a week, or chartering for longer periods.

Five experienced crew under the able command of Master John Cluett will show you the ropes of a tall ship.

The Jacques Cartier is fully equipped with electronic navigational aids, has three independent water-tight bulkheads to Board of Trade standard and carries complete life saving equipment.

Cabin accommodation is for 24 people in addition to the permanent crew of six, and comprises 2 x 4 berths, 4 x 3 berths and 2 x 4 berths.

Toilet and washing facilities include a shower bath. Those joining the vessel bring their own weather clothing as needed and for overnight sailing their own sleeping-bag or bed roll. All other equipment is provided.

Clubs, groups, schools, you as an individual or with your family and friends, can now participate in this exciting activity without prior training. Our crew, who can sail the ship if necessary without extra hands, will teach you the basics or specialist knowledge.

On overnight sailings you will have the opportunity of taking full part in the ship's routine, sharing the watches of 4hrs on and 8hrs off with the rest of the crew.

Men and women, boys and girls, the accompanied disabled, all are invited to take this inexpensive opportunity to set sail in a tall ship with its promise of adventure and the romance of past eras.

Rates:

1 Day Sail, adults £15.50, accompanied children under 14 £9.50.
Overnight Sailing (up to 4 days) adults £29.00 per person per day, accompanied children £19.50.
Full Week and over, adults £26.50, accompanied children £16.50 (price per person per day).
Special rates for Chartering on application.

All prices include victualling, personal accident insurance on board and automatic membership of the Channel Islands Seafaring Association.

For further information, reservations and advance booking contact:
Derek Stunes, Ship's Admin., Telephone (0481) 55839.
Les Vallees, Rue des Vallees, Castel, Guernsey, Channel Isles.

Participant in the Tall Ships Race.

59

Well, as the TV commercial says, "It just don't get no better than this."

I've been adopted by, and made honorary member of, the crew of the square-rigged tall ship, "Jacques Cartier." Even offered a job on the permanent crew this summer as they enter the Tall Ship Races. They are rounding up charts, navigation aids, and other things I will need to continue south when this nasty weather clears up. They also located and persuaded me to purchase a radio direction finder, then proceeded to teach me to use it. They didn't think much of my haphazard navigation technique.

Tonight, the committee that sponsors the ship is having a bar-b-que to which I have been invited. I didn't know that you could bar-b-que a sheep.

Chapter Eleven

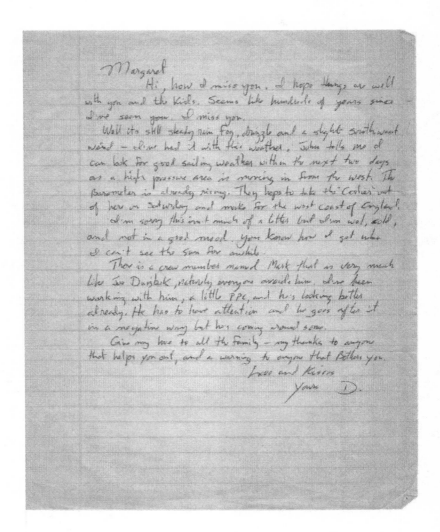

LETTER TO MARGARET

(Monday, June 24, 1985)

The weather hasn't improved any.

I have decided to buck the headwinds and squalls, catch the noon tide, and look for fair breezes somewhere else. They tell me a couple of hundred miles south, warm southerly winds and friendly currents always welcome you along the coast of Spain and Portugal. We'll see.

This has been a friendly port. Night before last, I had mutton b-b-que, raw fish salad, and a few other things I have never eaten before. Instead of Mesquite, the traditional fuel for the cooking fire is timber from wrecked boat hulls, which has about as pleasant an odor as our local cedar.

The host and hostess were school teachers on the island. Bob, the host, was quite proud of the fact that he had owned a horse and ridden with the wild cowboys from the Fiji Islands in the South Pacific, even producing a Fiji saddle that would have been impossible to stay in. Later, while everyone was singing sea shanties, he made an appearance in a native grass skirt and danced his own particular version of the hula, to the delight of everyone. Their sea songs and our older cowboy songs have the same tunes, for cowboys merely changed the words to fit the location.

Eventually, I was persuaded to sing "The Zebra Dun," accompanied by a French lady on the guitar, who was the wife of the captain of the "Jacques Cartier." Needless to say, it was different!

(Tuesday, June 25, 1985)

Yesterday noon, I said my goodbyes, exchanged gifts with friends, took a few pictures of the tall ship, and proceeded to set sail for the warmer coast to the south, against strong winds and good advice from the skipper of the Jacques Cartier.

With resolution, I clawed into the fierce headwinds, twelve-foot waves, and a list of 25 to 30 degrees – which my wife would say was well past the scream line – only to be thoroughly beaten back, and that night I limped back into the sheltered cove with my tail between my legs, wearily dropping anchor. I'll just call that a sailing lesson.

I'm back out in it this morning greeted by rain, fog, and barely enough wind to maintain steerage. After spilling my oatmeal down my leg this morning, I decided it's going to be another "one of them days!"

(evening)

After a day of going nowhere, rain coming down like the cow and the flat rock, I cranked up the engine and steamed back into port at St. Peter's, tying up rather sheepishly alongside the Jacques Cartier. If I can be this frustrated in twenty-four hours, what must it have been like in the old days, when at times they waited six weeks for a favorable wind to set off for the Americas.

Well, anyway, I paid my nickel and took my chances. Able hands and broad grins greeted my return as they helped me tie up the Swan. They had told me the weather was impossible, but I'm from Missouri!

(Friday, June 28, 1985)

I've been really sick the last couple of days, some kind of virus, I suppose. That plus the cold, the wet, and the lack of progress makes a fellow want to crawl into a sail bag and withdraw. It really makes me appreciate the hardships our ancestors endured to make it to the shores of America.

I'm feeling a lot better today. I wish I could say the same for the weather; it's still cold, rainy, and the wind straight out of the west. Although I've traveled several hundred miles in the last two days, my forward progress has been only eighty, but I'm proud of that eighty miles. I've clawed for every inch of it. Hopefully by dark, I can be around Ushant island (also known as Quessant, in French), west of Brest, France, and pick up a southerly course that will be compatible with these westerly winds.

The crew of the Jacques Cartier bid me bon voyage day before yesterday, with encouraging words such as, "How long will you be gone this time?" and "Should we keep supper warm for you?" They sure know how to send a sailor off!

I'm getting smarter. This boat has a long keel, so if you get your sails well set up, you can tie off the helm and hold a true course as long as the wind is fairly strong and doesn't change direction. This wouldn't work on my little Lake Belton boat.

Now, HAL, my autopilot, has just about lost his job and my batteries are getting a break. I had engine trouble as I approached Guernsey, so while in port, I used my Kim Blackman training and tackled the job. It turned out to be a clogged fuel filter, which wouldn't have been much of a problem had it not been located in the very innards of the Swan. Not being able to stand on my head for any length of time, I had to squeeze my big old body down through a locker and work in an area the size of a breadbox. I just knew that while I was in there, I would either get leg cramps or the boat would sink.

(Monday, July 1, 1985)

Caught my first fair wind yesterday and sailed happily for twenty hours into the Bay of Biscay, but not before spending the morning in a French version of Dante's Inferno. Cape de Quessant, the westernmost point of France, is a nightmare of dragon-toothed rocks, tremendous tidal flows, and the densest fog I have ever seen. Naturally, I caught them all just wrong.

I pulled down my sails, cranked up the Marstel engine, and shot those rapids in the fog like them two ol' boys bringing them chickens down the other side of "Wolf Creek Pass," or maybe Marilyn Monroe in the "River of No Return." Sometimes I could see or hear the rocks and avoid them. Other times, I just picked the widest narrow place and tiptoed through. After three hours of this sort of thing, the engine quit, the fog began to break, the wind picked up, and we sailed out into the Bay of Biscay, just like that was the way we had planned it all along. HAL stayed below with his head under a pillow. I renamed that Cape. (Cape Son of a Bitch)!

(afternoon)

It just doesn't get any better than this!

The cold and fog are gone, the sun is out, the black water has turned a beautiful pale blue, and I have a fair breeze straight over the stern. No tacking and beating into the wind – every mile I make is a mile nearer the coast of Spain, and the front gate of our place on Dodds Creek.

I wanted to put up the big spinnaker, as the breezes are light, but I've never set one before and haven't quite got the rigging all figured out yet, so I've got my main winged out to the port side, my working jib boomed out to the starboard, then my storm jib put up as a stay sail at the bow. I've never seen this done, but it sure works well. I may even have my laundry on the stern to get a little more push. She looks like a China Clipper. I've got HAL at the helm, so I can relax a little and absorb some more of James Michener's "Chesapeake." Hope he does as well on the Texas book he's working on. No worry, he hasn't written a poor book yet.

(Tuesday, July 2, 1985)

Sailed all night last night and all day today. Good steady wind out of the Northeast. Long day. May fire the cook!

(Wednesday, July 3, 1985)

The wind quit about three o'clock last night. This sleek, steady, stable, sailing vessel, the Swan, turns into an ugly duckling when the wind fails. It stumbles, staggers, roles, lurches, and weaves like a drunkard in the waves and swells.

On deck, getting the canvas down isn't too bad, as you have visual references such as the horizon, moon, etc. to help you balance.

Below deck, it's like a carnival Mad House – the wall slaps you in the face, the deck jumps out from under you, and you find yourself stacked in the corner, bent, stapled, and mutilated.

After twice being thrown from my bunk, I threw three sail bags on the cabin deck, wedged myself between them and the bulkhead, then instead of sleeping, I lay there and listened to all the gear I thought I had properly stowed, fall, roll, and tumble about the vessel. I don't think I got any of that REM sleep last night.

Oh, well, life's not all bad. This morning, I got three good readings from my Radio Direction Finder, shot my average maths, crossed my lines on the map, and there I was, in a little triangle sixty miles northeast of Cape Finisterre on the Spanish coast. Mrs. Milner would have been proud of me. Every now and then, it's nice to know where you think you are.

Of course, there are other good ways to navigate, like keeping the big tankers headed for Gibraltar on your starboard and listening to your radio to hear what language is being spoken predominantly. If you receive English, Dutch, German, Scandinavian, and French, you are somewhere in the Dover area. French and English means you're in the western part of the English Channel. French and Spanish puts you in the Bay of Biscay, and all Spanish puts you right here with me. When I start hearing Arabic from Morocco, it's time to turn right for the Americas. I wonder why no one has written a book on this type of navigation.

One thing I've learned about rock music. I can't understand it in other languages just as good as I can't understand it in English. This morning I heard the Lone Ranger on a Spanish station and was gratified to learn that "Hi Ho Silver" is the same in Spanish as it is in American.

(Thursday, July 4, 1985)

After four hard days and nights of sailing, I made the north coast of Spain. It's beautiful! Just like Mr. Hemingway said it would be. Rocky pine-crested hills, deep clear water, craggy cliffs, and a small fishing village with a calm anchorage, where I am going to get some much-needed sleep.

(Friday, July 5, 1985)

It's going to be a beautiful day. I've motored back out into Biscay, set my sails, and am patiently waiting for a breeze to spring up out of the north. I must have slept soundly, for all the fishing boats moored around me were gone this morning when I climbed out on deck. They are all around me out here, some running lines and others emptying lobster pots.

Some boisterous French fishermen woke me up one morning while I was drifting about the English Channel. They spoke no English, and my French is limited, so we got along fine. One kept offering me "whiskey." Well, I knew it was too early in the morning for that, so I used all my French in one burst.

"No Par la Vou" said I, whereupon he offered me two giant crabs, which I respectfully declined. They then decided I was crazy and roared off into the fog, laughing and shouting. Well, I knew I should've taken a crab or two, but I didn't know how to skin or cook one, and besides, them things looked plum dangerous making all that crackling noise and snapping their claws at you.

Now, if they had offered me something like the crawdads we used to get out of Hood Springs, well that would have been different. I can understand why, when Jesus needed some men to do a tough job, he picked fisherman. They are not afraid of the Devil himself, and give 'em a good boat, they'll sail to hell and back.

I would have liked to have gone ashore at that village last night, but being very tired and having no dinghy, I stayed aboard. I haven't been ashore in ten days; guess I'll wait for a port with a bank, post office, telephones, and an H-E-B.

I got my northeast breeze right over the stern. We are barreling down the Spanish coast with a lot of canvas up. I put up a big Genoa this morning – the first time I've ever used one – and it catches lots of air. I've sailed back onto my charts, thank goodness! When you sail off the edge of a chart and don't have the next one, it feels like you're sailing off the edge of the world.

I was advised in Guernsey to buy charts of the Bay of Biscay, but it's half as big as Texas and nothing but water, so I used my National Geographic maps to come across it. Besides, those big blank charts cost four pound, six pence each, and I'd rather buy groceries.

My east wind got better, then better, then too good! It turned into a gale. About ten tonight, I made it into a well sheltered port, dropped anchor, and fixed supper. Next thing I knew, I was drifting out to sea, as the wind had jerked my anchor loose. Now I'm back where I was, but I'll have to babysit this anchor a while to make sure it holds. I may have to put out a second anchor.

Definition of sailing: The art of staying wet and ill while going nowhere at great expense.

Chapter Twelve

(Saturday, July 6, 1985)

Slept with my teeth clenched last night.

Had to put out my second anchor at two o'clock, for my number one pulled loose. Then, spent the rest of the night eyeing the rock jetty fifty yards astern, wondering what action I would take if both anchors pulled loose in this gale.

I thought I was supposed to be safe in the harbor. I made a feeble effort to rig storm sails and pull out this morning, but I could figure no way to raise two anchors and stow the line, while managing the engine and tiller to stay off those rocks. So, I took a bath. I've never seen wind like this before. It's built to about forty-five miles an hour, no gust or slacks, just blowing straight and hard out of the north.

I broke out of the harbor this morning with my main reefed down to the size of a bandana and a storm jib up forward. I figured this would be a good opportunity to see what the Swan and me could handle. We didn't enjoy it, but I did get to experience some things I had only read about before.

I estimate the waves had built to about three times a man's height, and a lot of them were breaking. Others were having their tops blown off them. The Swan handles well in heavy seas; she's heavy enough not to be knocked about yet rides up and over the swells like the graceful bird she was named after. And, no, Margaret, she won't "tump over."

We had a hard run from Rio de Carme to another small fishing village called Camarinas, a distance of eighteen miles which we covered in about three hours. We caught two waves just wrong, with them breaking over the stern and flooding the cockpit. Needless to say, this dampened my enthusiasm, among other things.

At Camarinas, I dropped both my big Danforth anchors and still lost a hundred yards before they caught. We gained some ground and a lot of experience, but I believe I'll sit right here until this thing lets up.

(Sunday, July 7, 1985)

From one extreme to the other.

Today, the sea is glassy, with just enough breeze to irritate the sails and the sailor. A day like today would make Job cuss.

We did manage to pass Cape Finisterre, the western most rock in Europe, and it's all downhill from here to the Canaries. Spent the day finishing Michener's book, "Chesapeake," watching a herd of dolphins play, and envying the tankers on the western horizon moving at twenty knots or more. Tomorrow, with any luck at all, I'll make port at Bayona, where I hope to call home, get a bath, and some groceries.

(Monday, July 8, 1985)

It's been another long day.

It poured down rain, lightning everywhere, and hardly any wind at all. Static electricity started snapping and popping all over my rigging. I felt like a lightning rod stuck up out there and no place to hide. I finally picked up some formidable wind and sailed proudly into Bayona, just as Columbus did on the Pinta in 1493, after discovering the West Indies.

Spain seems to be a lot like Mexico; anything you want, they say, "mañana," but they tell me in Portugal, things are not that urgent. The banks are closed, and I've no pesetas, but I did manage to get a shower in the yacht club on credit. Told 'em I'd pay 'em – mañana. I guess after twelve days on this boat, they figured I could use it.

Downtown, everyone was eating seafood, steaks, etc., and I had to come back here and open a can of pork and beans. Sure were good, though. But wait 'til mañana!

July 9 1985
Bayona Spain

Darling
In a few hours I hope to get to talk to you. You
don't know how much I miss you. On my gloomy days
I use Thoughts of you and the kids to get me back
up. Hope you're all doing O.K. Give my love to the kids,
Mama and D.V.

Hope you and the horses and the cows are doing o.k. I am
sorry I left you with so much work.

Everyone tells me I'm to late to beat the hurricanes in the
Mid-atlantic and that I will have to lay over in the Canaries
until late Oct. or Nov. If it works out that way, I may
possibly fly home, as I can't see sitting around there that
length of time. Just some possibilities I'm considering.

Are you still at the same job and has it gotten any
better. Hope so.

Can't wait to talk to you. Sorry I'll probably wake you
up But I need it.

Love you Sunshine
Dean

P.S. Don't look for Bayona on the map. It's close to Vigo
in the Northwest part of Spain, only a few miles from the Portuguese
border. About Gabrielles size.

Love and Kisses

My two days in this city have been nice. Bayona is a clean town with a big fishing fleet, a castle, and lots of tourists. My favorite place was the fishing docks, where boats of all sizes, shapes, and colors make their way about daylight to unload and sort their catch. There are some strange-looking creatures in this ocean – and around here, they all get eaten.

From the docks, the women carry their baskets of fresh fish up the narrow rock lanes to the old town market (pescaderia) where loud and lively trading takes place. The men clean up their boats, get their nets ready for tonight, then off to the local bar, which apparently never closes. After some wine and loud bragging or complaints about the weather, it's off to bed, so they can do it again tonight.

At the market, after I bought some shrimp-looking crawfish, the lady demonstrated how they were to be eaten raw, with rapturous facial expressions and the licking of fingers. Well, I ate one, but let me tell you, they were much better cooked!

Near the town square, a group of ten or twelve hippies had set up shop, selling trinkets and getting people to sign a petition for some changes in the Constitution. Close at hand were about the same number of policemen, looking tough. The next day, a big disturbance took place there, and when I arrived, the hippies looked kind of beat up, their trinkets scattered underfoot, and the police looked innocent but smug. This is not Hyde Park.

(Friday morning, July 12, 1985)

I'm anchored in a small harbor just west of Viana do Castelo, Portugal, and here I'll stay until this fog lifts. I spent two days and one sleepless night wandering around in this soup, playing peek-a-boo with freighters, fishing trawlers, lost sailboats, and a rocky coast.

(13th July – Saturday)

Motored into port at Leca, with no wind and not much gas. It's been another bad day as Montezuma takes his revenge once more. I made it ashore in downtown where a big celebration was taking place but was unable to enjoy it with a stomach ache and no Portuguese escudos (money).

Margaret, don't throw away those Levi's that are thirty-four in the waist; I may be able to wear them again.

(Sunday, July 14, 1985)

Some days are diamonds, some are stones, and I was due for a diamond.

My diamond came in the unlikely form of William Afonzo, born in the Portuguese province of Goa on the west coast of India. Bill spoke five languages fluently, knew geography like Rand McNally, had been a ship's cook all over the world, and knew just the hotel to change my Spanish currency into something we could buy a little wine and roast chicken with.

We wined, dined, and saw the sites for less than three dollars total. That's what I call a bargain. Bill spoke English with an American accent he had picked up working near an American base at Stuttgart, Germany. He told me the big fiesta was in honor of the Portuguese fishermen killed in World War II. This didn't make too much sense, for I knew Portugal was neutral in the war. Bill explained that they were supposed to be, but it didn't always work out that way.

I intended meeting Bill back at the celebration tonight, but when I got back to the marina, a nice breeze had sprung up out of the north and the Swan was dancing to go. So was I. HAL is at the helm now, and we're making a good four knots down the coast towards Lisbon, Portugal.

Lately, statements of two of my heroes come to mind, and I try to follow their advice. One of his fellow Texicans was flabbergasted when he noticed Bigfoot Wallace asleep under a wagon during an Indian attack. Wallace explained his philosophy: "Eat when you can, sleep when you can – who knows when you'll get another chance."

And Ernie Pyle said, as he followed the infantry up the boot of Italy in World War II: "Never go anywhere without a roll of toilet paper."

Sewing sails

Chapter Thirteen

(Tuesday, July 16, 1985)

After leaving Leca, HAL, the Swan, and I sailed for twenty-four hours with a strong wind over the stern that grew stronger that night and the next day.

The swells had turned to mountains before we rounded Cape Carvoeiro and entered a well-sheltered port at Peniche, just about sundown. It took all hands and the cook to get the sails furled and the anchor down. I cooked some ham and eggs and fell into my bunk. HAL was asleep before the anchor caught, but the Swan danced all night and was ready to go again this morning. But she's a fifteen-year-old, and you know how they are.

I really slept good last night, in spite of getting up every couple of hours to check the anchor when some strange noise came up the anchor chain. I found this morning that the anchor was well dug into good sand, but the rode, or chain, was dragging across rocks and this turns my sleeping area into something similar to the insides of the base violin.

Peniche is beautiful. I had anchored in the lee of large cave-punctuated cliffs topped by a castle and surrounded by white-washed, red tile-roofed houses. I would have liked to have gone ashore, but with a strong favorable wind still blowing from the north, and not wanting to start the day with a cold swim ashore, I reefed in my mainsail, put up a small jib, and headed south. As Willie (Nelson) would say, "On the Road Again."

I made a good one hundred fifty miles yesterday, and with a little luck, I'll make Lisbon (Lisboa) today. I need to stock up with supplies there for my run to Morocco, on the African coast, and then to the Canaries. Yesterday, I seemed to be the only sailing boat out, but today another is running south with me. He is carrying only fore sails with his main furled, and as soon as we are separated a little, I'll change my sails to the same. I learn by watching.

(later)

Sure enough, when I changed my sails, I picked up a knot of speed, eliminated a lot of yaw, and did away with the danger of being clobbered by the boom if an accidental (Chinese) jib occurs. If things go wrong, the boom can come across like someone taking a swing at your head with a baseball bat. And if it put you overboard without your safety strap, HAL would sail on without you, never glancing back or even waving!

John, a British bloke, who furnished me dinghy transportation at Leca, said he didn't use a safety harness for he didn't want to have a "false sense of security." I assured him I wore mine all the time and had never picked up a false or any other feeling of security. Of course, John had a young couple sailing with him who might, or might not, sail back and pick him up.

Safety harness

76

(July ? 1985 – Lisbon, Portugal)

About the only thing I like about big cities is leaving them.

Well, maybe the streetcars are an exception.

Finding that Lisbon was too large to walk across, I took to the trams, which I love. They are like the ones in San Francisco now and Waco when I was a child. They have a funny system of fares. It seems that you can ride downtown free but have to pay to get back out. I only paid about thirty cents once and rode off and on all day.

I also learned to more readily appreciate Gatesville's banks. In one of the larger banks here, it took just over an hour to cash a traveler's check, and the paperwork would have choked a horse. The check made the rounds between five different desks, was kicked back twice, caused one loud argument, ground a quarter inch off my teeth, and completely wore out my fake smile. In Spain, it only took thirty minutes and wouldn't have taken that long if the cashier could have typed with more than one finger. I'm not complaining though, because that's one more finger than I can type with. I really wonder, though, how long it would take to replace lost traveler's checks…

There is a very good possibility that I will pick up a young Danish sailor from a neighboring yacht to accompany me to the Canaries. His ship is going into the Mediterranean, and he is wanting to go to the Caribbean, so we may work a deal. He has fifteen years of sailing experience and speaks better English than I do. With his years of experience and mine, that would give us a total of – let's see – nearly sixteen years!

(later)
(approximately July 20, 1985)

Somewhere along the way, I've lost track of the days and can't seem to backtrack well enough to re-date myself, so as Captain, I am declaring that today is 20th July for the crew of the White Swan.

I couldn't get a call through to Gatesville from Lisbon – maybe I'll have better luck in the Canaries. Every time I made it downtown to the overseas telephone exchange, they were closed for a three-hour siesta, and when they were open, there was no one at home at my home.

I lost the Danish deckhand before I ever got him aboard. It seems that all his mail from his girlfriend in the Copenhagen would be waiting for him at Gibraltar. I let him know that I wouldn't go that far out of my way to sign on Prince Henry the Navigator himself. After all, there's someone waiting on me, too!

I don't think I've met an unfriendly Dane in my life. This crew had me aboard for supper, and we made a much-needed paperback swap, for I was down to reading, "Tess of the d'Urbervilles," and although well written, it's not really my cup of tea.

Their engine was on the blink with no parts available until Gibraltar, so when we caught the tide out, I towed them down the Rio Tejo 'til we were clear of the banks. With a four-man crew and carrying lots of canvas, they soon left HAL and me in their wake as we headed down the coast toward the Cape of St. Vincent. My crew has learned the hard way – never put up more sail then you can get down by yourself, in a hurry.

After a twenty-four-hour run with a favorable wind, we passed Cape St. Vincent, the southwest corner of Europe, and plowed straight on for Africa. The tanker traffic was thick at the Cape, for all ships bound to or from the Mediterranean round this corner. After forty more hours out into the Atlantic, I've only seen one other ship, a giant Russian trawler coming out of the Mediterranean. At present, I'm about sixty miles north northwest of Casablanca and expect to make a landfall forty or fifty miles up the coast from Safi, Morocco.

(later)

It's been a long day with easy sailing in a fair wind, but still no sign of the African coast. If I've not made contact by late tonight, I will pick up a westerly heading to parallel the coast so as not to make contact with a crunch.

Margaret

I Miss you Sunshine
It seems like a hundred
years since I've seen you
but I think of you all the
time.

I'm in Lisbon — I'll try to
call you when I get ashore.
The last time I called I
tried to put it on VISA but
it had expired!

I'm in a hurry as my
neighbor is going ashore and I
am to ride in with him.

I'll call again when I get
to the Canaries.

LOVE
Dean

Chapter Fourteen

(July 21, 1985)

Changed heading to 230° MAG at 2300 hours last night, then back to 190° this morning. I got very little sleep, for the wind was from the North, and the swells were from the east. I was tossed about like a ping-pong ball until I crammed myself into a corner, and stacked things on top of me.

My radio says I'm very close to the African coast, for Radio Casablanca, a French station, is coming in very loud. Some of the stations are broadcasting in Arabic and some in what I take to be African dialects. The music is very interesting, although Radio Casablanca played nothing but Elvis Presley this morning.

(July 23 – I guess)

Happy birthday to my daughter Andrea – much love.

Seems I took a wrong turn and missed Africa. I have finally picked up a Morse signal on my RDF that tells me the Canaries lie on a heading of 230°, which I have already been using, so I'll just continue. I can't locate any other signals to cross reference for an exact location, but the station only has a range of 100 miles, so that should be pretty close to where I am.

As the man says, "Everybody's got to be somewhere."

This sure is a lonely ocean. I've only seen one fishing trawler since passing Cape of St. Vincent. I wonder where the traffic is that comes up the African coast going to the Mediterranean? Do you suppose they know something I don't know?

HAL has handled the helm for five days without even a coffee break. I think he's beginning to feel like he's the captain. My main concern is getting up the right canvas for the amount and direction of the wind, keeping it trimmed, and running the engine a few minutes every three hours, so HAL will have plenty of power from the batteries. Also, I have to cook and clean up after the whole crew, pump the bilge, do what little navigation that gets done, and stay on twenty-four-hour standby for emergencies.

For my leisure time, I have some second-rate books and Drew's radio. Quite a bit of the music I pick up is American, but a lot of it is nothing I've ever heard before. I heard a song a while ago called, "Buffalo Soldier Fighting in America," and I would sure like to have that record. It was on Radio Casablanca, a French language station, sung by a Jamaican, in English. It was obvious the singer couldn't speak English, though he did a great job of singing it, and the song lasted at least thirty minutes.

In Spain, I heard a rather long song about the sniper in the tower at Austin a few years back. Where they come up with these songs, I'll never know.

(July 24, 1978)

(I believe my dad became disoriented for about three days, due to the fact he put '1978' – Drew)

Another long uneventful day – ugh!

(July 25, 1978 (actually 1985))

Early this morning in heavy seas and poor visibility, I bounced off the coast of Africa. It didn't look very hospitable. The coast lay east to west, and as my charts showed only one such location, I once again knew where I thought I was. There were no ports of any kind anywhere within one hundred miles, so I took up a westerly heading with Fuerteventura of the Canarias to be my next landfall.

If my navigation is correct, I should reach there in about twenty-four hours. If it is incorrect, I will probably sail off the edge of the world. Also, the food on the ship is terrible.

(July 26, 1978 (1985))

Twenty hours after leaving Africa, with a failing barometer, failing spirits, self-doubt, homesickness, empty cupboard, empty stomach, and other problems, I hit Fuerteventura right on its beautiful lighthouse, and everything was OK again.

Not having slept in a horizontal position in several days, I put into the first small harbor I could find on the lee side of the island, dropped anchor, and climbed into my bunk. Three hours later, I was blown right out into the sea as tornado-like winds funneled down the valley and loosed my anchor. No rest for the wicked!

So, it's up storm sails, up anchor, and headed southwest down the lee side of the island. All day long, the wind would alternate between dead calm for twenty minutes, while the waves tossed you about uncontrollably, then blasts that put the gunnels underwater and washed the bottom third of the Swan's sails. Needless to say, HAL folded his one arm and let me take over.

At 6 p.m., we rounded the southern tip of the island, took up a 290° Mag. course that would take us just north of Gran Canaria, and on to Santa Cruz, on the Isle of Tenerife. The only change in the weather was that there were no more calms.

(July 27, 1985)

The Swan is heavy and doesn't beat up wind very well, so we were twenty hours to Santa Cruz on a west by northwest course, passing the light at Las Palmas de Gran Canaria around midnight and making the harbor at Santa Cruz about 4 p.m., a distance of about ninety nautical miles.

At the yacht club, where I expected a band to be playing and the crowd applauding my brave seamanship, I was greeted with a polite, "No, you can't moor your vessel here, as this is a private club; you will have to take yourself back up the coast five miles to the fisherman's harbor." Which was just all right with me, 'cause I liked the fishermen a damned sight better than that bunch anyway!

82

After an hour of motoring north through heavy seas, my engine began to cut out and died, just as I entered the harbor where some Spanish fisherman saw my problem and helped me tie up alongside a deep-sea trawler. After making repairs, I limped on to the little corner allotted to foreign yachts and tied up between two German brothers on my port side and an American girl from Indiana on my starboard. They helped me tie up at the bow, then one of the brothers in a dinghy carried my anchor out thirty meters astern and helped me set it. I adopted them all as fellow Texans on the spot.

(July 28, 1985)

Another diamond amongst the stones!

I borrowed enough pesetas to catch the bus to town, where a hotel clerk told me of a certain bar where I could change a twenty-dollar bill into something spendable, at a very poor rate of exchange. But I had been eating out of cold cans, and with a hamburger joint across the street, they had me! Why do I always hit port on Sunday when the banks are closed?

Next, I headed over to the docks, where the day before, I had spotted the biggest square-rigged sailing ship I had ever seen. It was a cadet training ship for future officers in the Venezuelan Navy, and they were having open house for the Governor of Tenerife. Well, I knew with my cowboy hat and boots they'd think I was part of the Governor's party, so I ambled aboard.

There were two-hundred-thirty men aboard, of which about half were cadets. The cadets gave tours around the ship, and I ended up with a Venezuelan, speaking to some Belgians in broken English – about like "Mex-Tex."

It was a beautiful ship. In light winds, they could put up twenty-three sails, ten-square rigged, and the rest stay sails and gaft rigged sails aft. She's heading back to South America tomorrow, and I hope to see her with her canvas up as she leaves.

I got attached to a young Belgium couple, and we spent the afternoon drinking cold drinks in the Plaza and discussing politics.

They told me President Reagan had been operated on for cancer, which I hadn't heard. All young Europeans that I talk with want to know why he is so tough on the Russians, and I counter with the fact that if America wasn't tough, they themselves would be speaking Russian, and they can't deny it. I've invited them to Dodd's Creek when they come to America to visit in a couple of years. If everyone I've invited shows up, I'll have to kill an extra hog!

Chapter Fifteen

(Monday, July 29, 1985)

This morning, I got downtown to Santa Cruz in time to see the Venezuelan clipper ship, Simon Bolivar, cast off her lines, hoist her sails, and head for home. As she left the dock, there were fifty-two white clad cadets at attention along the ten-yard arms high above the decks. It was a sight to see!

As she turned downwind outside the harbor, sail began to blossom until twenty-two sails could be counted. They figured to be home in eighteen days; wish I could make it that quick. The high point of the day, though, was getting my call through to home – but that's personal.

I had another young man come by this afternoon wanting to work his passage to the West Indies as a deckhand aboard the White Swan. He's from London's East End, the tough part of town, and has had no sailing experience but could learn fast, according to him. He looks pretty good and didn't back off when I gave him the negative side of what he could expect.

(Tuesday, July 30, 1985)

I've had no trouble at all sleeping at sea, being bounced around, but my three nights in port with a stable deck have netted me only nine hours of sleep. The moon is full, and I guess I'm moon-eyed. I've spent the morning buying groceries in Santa Cruz, and is that a chore!

To find nine items that you want, you have to go to five stores, each shop being about the size of a large room. After purchasing say fifty pounds of groceries, it's a half a mile to the bus stop afoot, a five-mile crowded ride, then another half-mile of hoofing down rocky trails to get to the fishing Marina. Then, if the tide is out, it's a twelve-foot climb down to the Swan's deck. If you have bought any smushable items, they did.

It hasn't been much better this afternoon with five half-mile trips afoot to the highway filling station for gas and to the fisherman's stinking showers for water, with five-gallon plastic jugs. This evening, I went to a small village north of here whose sandy beach was imported from the African Sahara.

The Scandinavian tourists must have bought their bikinis on sale, as most of them were "one-half off!" Needless to say, I left immediately!

Yesterday afternoon, I hiked about eight miles up a narrow canyon through banana groves, vineyards, and vegetable patches, built up behind stone walls to hold what little dirt is on this mass of volcanic rock. It looks exactly like the mountains in the heart of the Big Bend of Texas, dropped down into the middle of the ocean, then the edges sprinkled with fisherman and tourists.

Victor Gunn, the newest member of the crew, signed on tonight. He will move aboard tomorrow, and with any luck, we will be out of here the next morning with the tide. Being from London, Vic speaks no English, just some sort of Cockney that's impossible to understand. But I'll have him talking like a Texan after we are at sea a couple of weeks, or "mabe 'ill ave mue takin' laik em."

I think HAL likes him, as they are both limey blokes! While talking about navigation, I asked Victor if he could find the North Star. He said he'd try, but he didn't even know it was lost! Even HAL snickered.

(Saturday, August 3, 1985)

Well, things have taken a new turn, hopefully for the better.

In the fishing port at Santa Cruz, I made the acquaintance of a retired Danish sailor who had settled in the Canaries to avoid giving most of his savings to the Danish government, in the form of taxes. After visiting aboard the Swan and hearing of my plans, he advised me that my chances of making the crossing in this boat at this time of year were poor to none!

The best weather I could expect, he informed me, was high winds and heavy seas, and the worst was unthinkable, by which he meant hurricanes. Having sailed these waters for thirty years, for several American oil companies, he considered himself an expert and proceeded to tell me what I would be up against, if I persisted with this endeavor. He certainly didn't build up my morale any. But with a weak smile, I dismissed all this, setting my hand to the plow, and remembering the biblical promise of no reward to he, who after doing so, had occasion to look back.

After the second day of "the best weather we could expect," I reviewed my priorities, weighed them in the balance, and "looked back." In this "best weather," we could only manage a minimum sail. It was too rough for HAL, and Victor and I had to crawl and claw our way forward over a pitching deck, usually awash, to change sails or to pull them down altogether. Seasickness and exhaustion quickly took their toll, helping me to decide that all alternative courses of action should be decided upon.

Not being able to beat back up wind to the Canaries, I decided to run southeast to the coast of Africa, run south to Dakar or Gambia, and see if I could find a buyer for the Swan. This is our third day on the southeast course, and we hope to strike land somewhere near Villa Cisneros, a port on the southern coast of the Spanish Sahara.

As this was not on the trip itinerary, I have no charts for this coast and am having to rely on old National Geographic maps. I think the coast is the same, but the governments have all changed. I thought I was very knowledgeable in geography, but somehow, I am deficient on the west Coast of Africa.

(Sunday, August 4, 1985)

Happy birthday, Drew Anne, much love from your daddy. One day late.

The coast of the Spanish Sahara, so far, has been a bleak and desolate place. After running down the coast for twenty-four hours, we have seen no buildings or any signs of civilization, just mountains of sand and mesa like hills. Heavy winds, a lee shore, large swells, and low clouds have made this a dreary day, not being improved by a graveyard of three oceangoing ships, the skeletons of which protrude from the sands and surf a mile off our port side.

Victor is making a willing hand and seems to pick up things quickly, although I still cannot communicate with him in his own language, which is London street language. He fixed breakfast this morning, and being British, we had sardines and toast, which wasn't half bad.

Below the Spanish Sahara is Mauritania, a large country inland which seems to be made up mostly of desert. My Portuguese chart shows only one port on its coastline, that being Port-Etienne, on the lee side of the Cape Branco. Next comes about one hundred and fifty miles of coastline in Senegal, of the Federation of Mali, of which Dakar must be the capital. The only other name I recognize in this country is the fabled city of Tombouctou (Timbuktu), over a thousand miles inland; then Gambia, which is or was, a part of the British Empire. Here I hope to make some sort of deal on the Swan – either making a huge profit or taking a bigger loss – purchasing a one-way airline ticket to Texas and heading back to paradise!

(later)

Once again, we know where we are, Villa Cisnaros, a port in the Spanish Sahara. After rounding the Cape and dropping anchor near a small Arab village, I swim ashore to ask our position of the locals. They could speak French and Spanish and me a little Mexican, so I was able to locate the port, some ten miles due north against a twenty-knot wind. We tried but didn't make it.

After dropping two anchors, building supper, and starting to relax after four straight days and nights of sailing, we quickly went back on emergency duty, for the boat began to bump the bottom as the tide went out.

We are now at a hopefully safer depth, but surely something else will happen to spoil a good night's sleep. I believe I prefer my old pickup truck, in which you can turn off the ignition, set the brakes, and usually it will be right there the next morning, even if one of the tires might have gone a little soft.

Dean on board the Swan (notice the growing beard!)

(Monday, August 5, 1985)

So much for my good night's sleep – you'd have to see it to believe it.

Just as it got dark, and I had climbed into bed, a semi-destroyer roared out of the night, began circling the Swan as ten or twelve of its pirate-looking crew shouted in French, Arabic, and Spanish, flashing searchlights and throwing lines across our deck – us not knowing whether to grab the lines or to stand by to repel boarders!

As the aggravating ship was a military gray with what looked like a twin fifty-caliber machine gun mounted on the foredeck, I decided on a plan of complete cooperation, making HAL put away his belaying pin and assisting as several Moroccans swarmed aboard and commenced to tie the Swan to the stern of their vessel.

We were ordered to pull up the anchors. I got the forward one in, but three of us couldn't get the big second Danforth anchor loose at the stern. I was told to cut the rope, which I respectfully declined to do. I was ordered to cut the line a second time, so with my trusty Schrade Walden, I cut loose one hundred and fifty dollars' worth of anchor, chain, and line, while muttering a prayer that Allah would grant them eternal torment from the fleas of a hundred camels!

Through wild winds and seas, the Swan was dragged about ten miles to the port of Dakhle, while one crew member stayed aboard to practice English on me as I parried in my best Spanish. In the military basin, we were tied up alongside a rusty barge, then boarded and interrogated by a half-dozen military officers. Some of the questions were about the boat, others were about John Wayne and Charles Bronson, some also about country music. At around two o'clock in the morning, they said everything was okay, that this was normal procedure, and with much goodwill and handshaking, we were un-boarded. I didn't get much sleep.

At daybreak, the customs people showed up to have coffee, search the ship, wonder where my ships papers were, and again pronounce everything okay, in broken English.

At two o'clock, a military group showed up with a long list of handwritten questions, stayed an hour, searched the boat, and again pronounced everything okay. No wonder we are the only foreign vessel in port. Now, all we have to do is get permission to leave, if the wind ever drops below forty knots!

We managed to get a military pass to get off the naval base and downtown, but there wasn't much going on there. Everything was very cheap, but there wasn't anything to buy. This afternoon, we were asked to move our boat from alongside the barge to another point on the quay. This was near impossible in forty mile-an-hour winds, but we managed to tie up again, and now it looks as if we'll spend the night tending our warps as the tide falls and being bounced about by the swells.

Things are looking much better this afternoon, as everyone who has learned English in military school comes by to practice on us, and we on them. The tugboat captain invited me aboard his vessel for coffee and spent an hour showing me courses and channels on his charts to help me get safely to Dakar. His engineer carried me through the ship, being very proud of its twin USA Caterpillar diesel engines and the excellent shape of the vessel. Upon leaving, I was given two jugs of mineral water and about three pounds of squid, which were the first I have ever tried, and they made an excellent supper.

Just at dark, we were again ordered to move the Swan to another location as a fifty-caliber machine gun was set up on the quays end, and we were in their field of fire. This move was accomplished in high winds and large swells, resulting in some damage to the Swan and completely demolishing my self-control. I gave them all a loud, old-fashioned Texas cussing, and hoped they had an interpreter to translate every word! I think they caught the general meaning.

(Tuesday, August 6, 1985)

The local bank wouldn't cash a traveler's check or exchange foreign currency. After an hour wait, I did manage to get a call through to Gatesville on one of the old hand-crank telephones. I heard at least ten words from Margaret and Drew, and hope they understood as many from me.

After saying goodbye to a few friends, we pulled out of Dakhla, heading south and hoping to make Dakar in six days. We did as Paul and his fellow evangelist did upon leaving towns where the welcome was poor – we shook off the dust from our sandals and swore never to return.

Usually in this type of weather, the sea looks dangerous and forbidding, but today it was a relief to get out of that port and back into the clean ocean. For supper, we had chicken-fried squid.

(Wednesday, August 7, 1985)

We had a good day's run since leaving Dakhla, probably making over one hundred miles the first day. The wind has been directly over the stern, gradually increasing until reaching gale force this afternoon, obliging us to pull down everything but the storm jib, and prepare to spend the night being slewed about by the giant swells.

(Thursday, August 8, 1985)

Good steady winds. We sailed with maximum sail and made good progress. In the afternoon, an ocean-going Soviet trawler pulled up alongside the Swan and looked us over, then sailed away.

Chapter Sixteen

Today has been rather lazy, with an indifferent northerly breeze.

About two o'clock last night, we were entertained by a school of dolphins doing singular and group acrobatics beneath and around the boat, leaving twenty-foot fiery wakes of glowing phosphorus in their trails.

Also today, we noticed in our wake – fins. We, at first, took them to be shark, but they turned out to be a very large herd of killer whale, which I would guess to number at least a thousand. The leaders were surfacing all around the Swan, and the pack fanned out in a wedge shape in our wake for a half-mile or more astern. It looked as if our noble craft, with flags flying, was leading this army of charging, snorting, blowing, mammals into dubious battle!

They behaved very similar to our Gulf of Mexico porpoise, being somewhat larger and darker and having a rather ungainly round head with a white underside. They stayed an hour, and then departed.

With fair winds, we are about two-and-a-half days' north of Dakar, running straight south. What we will do there depends upon what conditions we find. It being the capital of Senegal and a large city, I hope to find a market for the Swan and air transportation home – but I wouldn't bet on it.

I have no idea the language spoken there nor the type of people we will encounter – this makes it interesting!

With the Swan lazing along at two knots and no fins in sight, I decide to take a swim, as it is a very warm day. With a bowline knot around my chest and a safety line secured to the stern cleat, I dropped over the stern of the Swan, not worrying about hitting the bottom, as the chart showed it over two miles down.

93

The current immediately took my swimming trunks, which I managed to save and throw aboard, then dragged me along at a very fast clip, making me decide that about two minutes would be plenty for my Friday night bath. After struggling back aboard, using loops of rope especially laid out for that purpose, I have concluded that to go overboard accidentally in even moderate sailing weather would make it nearly impossible for a person to get back aboard by himself, if not impossible.

As most of our fresh fruits and meat have been eaten up, tonight we will dine on an old TDC (Texas Department of Corrections) recipe, chicken-fried bologna. My old, weather-worn National Geographic map shows the area south of Dakar to be jungle, so maybe bananas and pineapple will again be abundant, as they were in the Canaries.

There was nothing fresh in Dakhla, except some bundles of green alfalfa. The potatoes and onions were dry and must have been shipped in, for there was nothing around but miles and miles of sand. We did buy some bread, but that was a mistake.

Slow sailing days are hard on me – I clean, tinker, and repair, but still the day is long. If I hadn't been able to purchase an overpriced copy of Charles Dickens' "David Copperfield" in Tenerife, I would probably be pulling my hair out. As it is, it's just falling out of its own accord.

(August 10, 1985)

We are becalmed and adrift on a glassy sea, our sails worrying themselves to tatters, as the Swan rolls in the swells, about a half-mile off the coast of Africa, maybe eighty miles north of Dakar, seemingly a port too far.

This morning, we were treated to our first severe squall since Victor has been aboard, and though he is a personable young man and good company, he is no sailor, retreating below decks to his bunk to sleep out the storm. I am glad I learned this here and not in a severe depression in mid-Atlantic. The sea is a hard taskmaster, teaching patience and trying patience in the same lesson, laying problem after deadly problem before its inept pupils in an impersonal manner, caring not or not capable of caring a wit whether the student survives the lesson or not.

As for myself, I think I have been out here too long. Being separated from the ones you love makes you realize their worth more clearly and what would be forfeit by a failure to return. Wives, mothers, daughters, and granddaughters are much too precious to be neglected over long periods of time.

(August 11, 1985)

We have been caught like a fly in the clenched fist of that awful creature, "the Doldrums."

Unable to escape, we fry on the griddle of the mirror-like sea, in the fierceness of the Sahara-heated African sun. Not a ripple of wind to cool a sweat-soaked body, sprawled under a make-do tent of useless sail on the foredeck, covered from head to sun-darkened toe with salt water-rotted Levis and bleached chambray shirt, as protection from this oversized microwave.

Master Victor Gunn, lately of East London, is standing on the aft deck, debating the pros and cons of a cool swim. The cons, I think, being his reluctance to offering himself as bait to some of the rather large fish we sometimes observe lying in the shade of the Swan. I think to myself, the longer the debate, the less likely a swim.

I have finished "David Copperfield." I slowed my reading to make that masterpiece last, much as a desert wanderer conserves his last few swallows of water, hating to see the end of it. But it's gone "by Gorme," as Mr. Peggotty would have said – Mr. Dickens having wrapped it all up rather neatly.

Day before yesterday, we were overtaken by ten or twelve black African fishermen in a very long, beautifully-painted, seagoing canoe with an inboard engine. They seemed to speak French and were requesting through sign language, something to drink from a bottle.

95

Being well-acquainted with the wants of French, Spanish, and Portuguese fisherman, I tried to explain that I had no beer aboard. "No beer – agua" was the reply, so we tossed them a gallon jug of water, for which we were well-thanked in many languages, as they roared off to where ever it is fishermen go.

African fishermen

(August 12, 1985)

The wind freshened yesterday evening about four, and very soon after dark, we were able to make out the Cape Verde light, although we were still a long way from it.

This morning, we are beating into a contrary headwind after a long night of the same. We are on the northern edge of Dakar, needing only about five miles to round the Cape and make for the harbor on the southern side, but I am afraid we will be many hours accomplishing this, for we are bucking a very persistent headwind.

Dakar's airport is very busy, and the city's skyline seems to be that of a busy modern town, as opposed to the round grass huts of native villages we observed further up the coast. The beach is rocky with some sandy inlets lined with red tile roofed buildings, also some roofed with palm leaves. The Cape is very beautiful, but the rusting hulls of two large ocean-going freighters twisted among the rocks just north of the light, remind us to pay attention to business and tack north again.

(August 15, 1985)

What an experience this part of Africa has been. It is at once, very beautiful and very dirty, rich in ways and very, very poor in others. I have met some very fine people, some pickpockets, a thousand handicapped beggars, and some who would give you the very shirt from their back – in all, it's an interesting place, but let the traveler beware!

Me, the old-world traveler, after taking much precaution, had my front Levi's pocket picked as clean as a Christmas turkey by an African magician. Luckily, his hand netted only a couple of traveler's checks, an expired Visa card and a Texas driver's license which he probably can't use anytime soon. Come to think of it, I also lost my library card, blood donor card, V.F.W. membership certificate, and Drew's telephone number.

Heck! I eased on down to the American Embassy for a little help and information, where the reception I received once again made me very proud and thankful to live under the protection of "Old Glory," which even with its many faults, in my eyes stands head and shoulders above any other nation I've seen, bar none.

There's a French couple with four small children moored near the Swan who have really been helpful in many ways, making this – in spite of putrid water, millions of dead fish, and other unmentionables – a good port. The husband, Robert, built their boat, and they are on a three-year trip that will end in the Caribbean next year – brave souls! Ani, the mother, speaks fair English, not enough for American citizenship, so I have declared the whole family "fellow Texans," and naturally invited them to come to Dodds Creek when in the United States, which they seem to think they might accept. I'm also volunteered as official babysitter.

If anyone runs into Karl Malden, tell him to do his next American Express commercial in Dakar and see how quickly he gets his stolen traveler's checks replaced. I've been to the police; they need two days to get a form to fill out, to carry to the travel agency, to even start the process. I'll wait and see, but Karl, I'm afraid it just ain't so!

There seems to be no market at all in this area for a sailing yacht, so once again I'm stocking up groceries, water, and fuel with the intentions of setting out west to the Cape Verde islands, then on across to the West Indies. I intend to travel alone, for it is much easier to take care of your own wants and needs in the confines of the Swan, without having to consider the requirements of another crew member.

Today is a local holiday, so tomorrow will be the day I again make an assault into the downtown area to post some mail, phone home, and promptly be reimbursed for the lost checks. A Canadian couple came by a minute ago and invited me to an American club later this evening. It sounds very good, for they are showing an old Western movie and have real hamburgers.

How could I possibly resist that!

Chapter Seventeen

I fought my way through obstinate taxi drivers 'til I located the American club – a rented guesthouse behind someone's villa with a snack bar, tennis court, and swimming pool – and the snack bar served REAL hamburgers!

There were very few Americans about, most of the people being from other diplomatic Embassies. I struck up a conversation with a Tunisian who worked for some international aid agency. He seemed rather anti-American, and we seem to have little in common, until we started discussing books, then it turned out that our favorite authors were the same. Melville, Conrad, Michener, Hemingway, and others, which carried us on 'til we got into old movies, of which he was a great fan.

He knew every actor and most of the dialogue of the old greats such as Red River, Darling Clementine, Gunfight at the OK Corral, Casablanca, and on and on. Later, he invited me to his home where, although he could possibly be a concert pianist, his proudest piece of music was "Red River Valley," from the movie, "Red River," laboriously picked out with one finger and a happy smile. Tonight, he is taking me to a lobster supper and a movie at the club, and over the weekend, I'm taking him sailing in the islands near here.

About traveler's checks – the police told me to come back Monday for the paper I need. I said, no, I had to have it now – so they typed it out and gave it to me! The agency where I went to be reimbursed treated me like I was dirt, but did manage to get the job done, sending me then to the bank, where I waited an hour to get the cash. But money in the pocket sure feels good in a port such as this one.

It cost a lot, but I got my call through home – it was worth a lot!

See you soon!

(Saturday, August 17, 1985)

The Marina that HAL, the Swan, and I call home is primarily designed for a fleet of boats that carry sport fisherman out to fish for sailfish. It would be a rather nice place – palm trees, cabañas, and such – if the water in the Bay wasn't clogged with sewage, dead fish, and dead flip-flops.

Also, the Swan is forced to lie on her port side at a twenty-degree list when the tide is out. Anyone trying to sleep must compensate periodically for this or fall out of their bunk.

In port, I am able to get only one or two hours of sleep a night at the most, usually lying on the foredeck with a light blanket over me, covering everything but my nose – which I coat with mosquito repellent. I really think they use the odor of the repellent to zero in on my location. The blanket is rather warm in this superheated humid atmosphere, but it sure beats trying to sleep below, where there isn't a breath of air stirring, and the mosquitoes can make their diving attacks without the interference of crosswinds and turbulence.

There have been heavy rains the last two nights, and there is hope among the Aid workers here that the drought in this area is over. Dakar, as large as it is, has no drainage system, and all the trash built up over long periods floats around in the deep water in the middle of the streets, stirred by naked children playing, laughing, and enjoying the water's coolness.

(Sunday, August 18, 1985)

Vic Gunn, my temporary shipmate, departed this morning to the airport to catch a Pan Am flight to New York where he has friends, then south to the Bahamas. I wish him luck. There's nothing wrong with him that won't be cured by thirty years of hard work and experience, but that's another story.

My Tunisian friend will be here at noon today, and if the wind will blow, we'll take a ten-mile sail out to an island that once was a prison and now is a resort. I cannot remember his Arabic name or pronounce it, so I call him "Red River" after the old movie, this suiting him just fine.

Yesterday, at the American club, where I retreat often for a breath of fresh English, I met an English couple, lately of Switzerland and Canada, who just recently arrived here to work with World Vision's relief efforts in this area. Margaret and I had helped support this agency for about a year, and it was especially interesting to me to hear of their projects in this area, for most of the publicity is centered around Ethiopia, much further to the east. I was pleased to learn that half their efforts were spent on feeding destitute people; the other half being used on long-term projects to help the people re-establish their self-sufficiency, mostly through improved agriculture and the elimination of the self-defeating slash and burn type of farming now practiced.

We had observed on our trip down the coast, a strip of forest, hand-planted in rows that stretched several hundred miles north of Dakar. I was told by a Canadian Aid worker that this was a project to reclaim the coast line from the advancing Sahara, and that it seemed to be working very well. I would really like to get inland and talk to the people who actually run the projects, instead of the paper shufflers here in their air-conditioned offices, but it is impossible to leave the Swan alone at night without her being assaulted and stripped by some of the local harbor pirates. Twice, I have rousted boatman that were alongside at three in the morning, feeling along the Swan in the pitch black for ropes, anchors, clothing, or anything that was movable. So far, I think I have only lost my swimming trunks to them.

(Tuesday, August 20, 1985)

My Irish blood seems to be paying off lately, as my luck improves each day.

I received some money from home through the American Embassy, they being very helpful and cooperative, especially a Mrs. Anderson, who went to bat for me. She also furnished me with a

101

name and business address of an American Aid worker, another sailing nut, who promptly took me in tow.

Between us, we worked out a plan and located a place to leave the Swan until December, when the hurricane season is over, and the trade winds are ambling along peacefully toward the Caribbean. My new-found friend, Norman Revkin of upstate New York, then carried me home with him to a dinner party he and his wife were giving for some friends, things becoming more homey when one of the wives turned out to be from Austin, Texas.

Norman's wife is a fine woman – Danish, with a name I could not remember, or pronounce, if I could. She again reinforced my conviction that I had never met a Dane I didn't like, both insisting I spend the night in their government-furnished mansion with hot and cold running water, real beds, electric lights, no tides or Moroccan pirates, and an air conditioner in my bedroom. The room rolled with the swells a couple of hours until I put on the lights. Then it stopped, and I went promptly to sleep. It just don't get no better than that.

After leaving Norman at his office this morning, not before adopting his wife and himself as fellow Texans, I proceeded to Air Afrique, where I learned I could fly out of here to New York for around four hundred dollars aboard a freighter with a few passengers scattered somewhere inside. I held off buying a ticket until I proceeded to the Beaujolias to check out another option – but that's a whole another story, and it's getting dark!

(Wednesday, August 21, 1985)

Now the rest of the story …

I've been fortunate in making friends with many of the crew of the tanker, Beaujolias, in port to discharge a large amount of cracked rice to the hungry people further inland. The Captain, Jerry White from upstate New York, had one time taught sailing at the military academy, so naturally he was interested in my amateurish efforts getting from there to here by sail.

The first mate, a Lufkin Texan transplanted from Cairo, Egypt and speaking Gyp-Tex is a heck of a nice guy and has certainly made me feel at home aboard the Beaujolias. In fact, he has fed me a couple of meals at the officer's mess that were excellent, even if I had not been eating cold vegetables out of cans for days.

But the big surprise in this bunch was Chuck La Monie, the company representative who flew in for the off-loading of the Beaujolias. Chuck has a thirty-mare horse farm in Folsum, Louisiana, and while not knowing Jack and Mary Marvitch personally, he knew the place and all their horses and of Jack being killed in the car wreck. When he drug out the Quarter Horse Journal, I wished Margaret were here, as she knows most of its chapter and verse.

Chuck was going to contact the company today and see if it would be possible to put the Swan aboard the Beaujolias on its return trip to the U.S. That would be great, but I think it would be too much to hope for. But if you don't ask, you never know.

The captain and some of the crew are coming by here this afternoon, and we intend to sail out to an offshore island near here for some clean swimming and sightseeing. The weather is good, and the wind is right, so I hope they show up.

Chapter Eighteen

(Thursday, August 22, 1985)

Today, I bought the ticket that will take me to New York, from where I will fly to Houston, get my pickup from my old friend, C.F. Lively, and turn it northwest until I cross the waters of the Dodds Creek. There, I will kiss the ground – after kissing Margaret – and vow never to do anything like this again until December!

Dakar is a hard town – let the traveler beware.

At the travel agency where airline tickets are purchased, I had been quoted a price of four hundred dollars for a ticket to New York, via Air Afrique. Today, when I went to pay for it, the price had mysteriously jumped to six hundred and fifty dollars, with the four-hundred-dollar price not again to be available until the middle of September. I picked up my gear, told them that was fine, I would find my own airline ticket home even if I had to go through China. My agent then, with many pardons, great skill, and perseverance, worked it out with the airline to carry me for just under the original agreed-upon price. My, my, how strange things work in this part of the world.

I also visited Sean Fitzgerald at the American Embassy, who has a fishing boat in the Marina where we moor, who agreed to keep an eye on the Swan until I come back for it. Also, I intend to hire a local to sleep aboard at night to hopefully keep the pirates from sacking and plundering the poor old Swan and HAL. HAL wanted to come home with me, but he didn't have a passport.

Yesterday evening, the skipper of the Beaujolias, Jerry White, Chuck La Moine, and the third engineer, Craig something, spent the afternoon sailing the Swan about the bay and out to the Ile De Goree, while I settled back to watch and learn.

Jerry, I found out today, has been a world-class ocean racer, and Craig, though much younger, wasn't far behind in his ability to make the Swan sit up and do her stuff. She didn't act like the same boat, but more like the old violin, in the poem, that was battered and scarred but still responded to the "touch of the Master's Hand." I watched closely, asked questions, and learned a lot. They put up sails I didn't even know were aboard. Jerry showed me how to rig the mainsail for jiffy reefing instead of roller reefing, thereby doing in thirty seconds what it was taking me ten minutes (or being impossible) to do in rough seas.

We sailed out to Goree Island, which is beautiful, and enjoyed a swim until we were forced to up anchor, to escape the multitude of kids that swarmed aboard, bent on removing anything movable from the decks of the Swan. Those little rascals would swim out by the hundreds to meet the ferry and hang all over it like barnacles as it approached port. I'm sure there must be a lot of them killed each year, as they would swim between the jetty and the boat as the swells slammed into the wall of rock.

When we returned to port, we went aground well outside the Marina and there dropped anchor. A French friend of mine came out in his dinghy and carried my friends ashore, while I settled down to wait for the midnight high tide, finally getting the mooring ropes around the Swan's neck at about 11 o'clock. With a strong onshore wind that only the toughest mosquitoes could buck, I got the first halfway decent night's sleep I've had since coming to this dubious port. On the foredeck, I covered myself with a blanket, put repellent on ears, forehead, and nose, and tried to sleep, although some of the varmints try to claw their way through my beard.

Tomorrow, I'm taking several more crew members of the Beaujolias sailing, as they have been four months aboard the ship and are feeling the strain. I repay myself by frequenting their mess, which is the best place in Dakar to eat that I know of.

(Saturday, August 24, 1985)

A couple of nights ago, my family of French friends aboard a nearby yacht had me over for supper and French lessons. We had a great time, and I learned pretty fast for an old country boy who only knew one expression in their language, that being "French fries."

The kids had studied English in school but were too shy to try to speak it, though they were quick to catch any mistake their mother made. Anni, Mrs. Bizon, is a retired schoolteacher, though she doesn't look over thirty, while Robert, the husband, is a woodworker and a boat builder, having built their yacht into a beautiful floating home.

This morning, as I was battening down the Swan, I called them over and loaded their little rubber dinghy with food that would probably spoil or be stolen if left aboard. They returned shortly with a beautiful African glass painting that I would really like to carry back with me, but with it being very fragile, I had to leave it behind.

I cleared the Swan, locked her up, stored some gear in the Marina office, and headed down the road to the Beaujolias, where I figured I could put up at least one night.

Sure enough, I was welcomed aboard, but it was like going from the frying pan into the fire, their air-conditioning having broken down. It is fiercely hot, with at least a dozen big diesel engines roaring, as they drag rice out of the holds on conveyor belts and move it ashore, where it is sacked by several hundred Africans and hauled away. Everything within a quarter mile is covered with white dust from the rice, and if you sweat a lot like I do, you begin to look, after a while, like a walking tortilla. The nearest thing I've seen to this is working on the old-time thrashers out on the Schloeman farm west of Gatesville in the fifties – the good old days!

Yesterday, I carried eight or ten Beaujolias crew members sailing, finally dropping anchor about three hundred yards off the beach, just after dark. A small boat came out and carried several in, the rest of us swimming ashore against a strong tide.

After a meal at a French restaurant on the beach and a long bull session, it was time for me to swim back to the Swan. It was very dark, and the only way I could locate her was to keep her between me and the lights of some Russian trawlers anchored about five miles out in the bay. That morning in the marina, I had seen two eight-foot Tiger sharks brought in and hung up by some fishermen. As I swam toward the Swan, I began to get the feeling I had company in the black waters around me, this feeling intensifying until I could almost hear the throbbing music from "Jaws" – Boom Boom Boom Boom, Boom Boom. After about twenty minutes, I reached the boat and got aboard much quicker and easier than ever before.

After sailing back to the Marina, I hung around on my anchor and fed the mosquitoes until the tide would let me get back to my mooring. Even in the stifling heat, with my blanket up to my nose, the deck awash with sweat, and Kamikaze mosquitoes working on my ears, I slept fairly well, except when I would be awakened by the background music from Jaws.

(Sunday, August 25, 1985)

One more day and I might be flying home.

I know better than to get my hopes too high, as in this part of the world, whatever can go wrong, usually does. I wish every young person in America could spend some time over here, not in the tourist resorts where you are pampered, but in the real world where these people must work and exist. I think that two things would become very clear: one being that we should aid these Third World countries in their efforts to improve their living standards; and two, and most important, that America has developed a unique society based upon individual freedom that is, yes, worth fighting and dying for, to preserve for generations yet unborn.

(Tuesday, August 27, 1985)

"If it weren't for bad luck, I'd have no luck at all," as the words of the song go.

My fare was paid. I was to pick up my ticket at the travel agency at four o'clock Monday afternoon and be on a flight out of here at midnight, but no one bothered to tell me Monday was a holiday, and also today – and the travel agency wouldn't open on those days. I can't believe this place.

107

I'll bet there has never been a tourist that has ever made a second trip to Senegal. I know one Texan who won't.

While waiting and hoping the agency would open yesterday evening, I watched trios of pickpockets try their luck with anyone who came downtown, the local police ignoring them as if they had a perfect right to steal anything they could. Everyone here who I have had dealings with is into some kind of racket, shakedown, kicked back, bribes, etc. Even aboard the Beaujolias, to get the rice unloaded for the starving inland, certain bosses and pushers have to be continually paid off or the unloading mysteriously slows down or even stops.

I noticed an article on Senegal and Dakar in the National Geographic the other day. I looked at the pictures but didn't have time to read the story. If it said anything good about Dakar, we apparently haven't visited the same places.

The Captain, Jerry White, and the crew of the Beaujolias, are the only bright spots I have seen lately in this ungodly port. If not for their welcome aboard, my small amount of cash would already be used up, leaving me stranded in New York, if I ever get there. What with the severe heat and being very weak from African diarrhea, my spirits are at rock bottom, and my sense of humor, which I can usually get cranked up, won't even turn over. Although I would love to be working, and the ship's crew could use the help, company rules prevent me from making a hand aboard the Beaujolias, adding a sense of uselessness to the frustration I already feel. Oh well, things could be worse, and probably will be.

Watching the crew of the Beaujolias, you understand what sets America somewhat apart from other nations. This old ship, which was built in 1954 – the year I graduated from high school – has had a continual string of severe problems since docking here in Dakar. Air-conditioning has gone out, water purification systems fouled, electrical generators burned up. Still, this bunch just works harder, gets greasier, nearly fry trying to get a little sleep, and keeps smiling. They have a good captain, and they know it – he also knows he has a good crew.

(Wednesday, August 28, 1985)

If luck is with me, I could be out of Africa tonight, but as Lady luck has been rather shy lately, I try not to build my hopes up at all.

(later)

This has been a day I will always remember, although I would rather not.

My friendly travel agent apologized to me, upon arrival at his office, for forgetting that Monday and Tuesday were the biggest holiday of the Muslim world, celebrating Abraham's offering of a goat to the Lord, instead of his son. He then assured me he would get me aboard an Air Afrique flight out of Dakar Friday night, and that I should come back tomorrow and pick up my ticket.

After explaining rather strongly that I would have a ticket or my money returned before I left the office, and that the police and the American Embassy would be brought in, my agent set off to the Afrique office to get the ticket.

Shortly, he returned with a worried look on his face, explaining that the flight was booked full, and he was having trouble recovering my money which had already been turned over to Air Afrique. After an hour and a half's work, he finally came back from the airplane office with my refund, less 10,000 francs tax, and the money he brought back was in French francs, not Senegalose as I had paid with. I had no idea what a French franc was worth. My stomach was boiling, my teeth were grinding, and I was seeing red!

An hour after the office had closed, we finally found a Pan Am flight out at two-thirty tomorrow morning, this costing another two hundred dollars of U.S. and Senegalese money, which I had intended to use to get from New York to Houston. To heck with Houston – just let me get out of this place and back to the good ol' U.S.A.!

Back at the Beaujolias, the ship was being moved up the dock to permit another tanker loaded with grain to use the deepest end of the quay. As the engines are still down and there was no steam aboard, the captain had to use a tugboat for moving up and Norwegian steam to handle the very large and very heavy lines ashore – Norwegian steam being a line of about ten men hauling on the wet ropes.

I was finally permitted to lend a hand and fell to with a will. It was hot, hard, and heavy work, just what I needed to get some of the poison out of my system. Cooks, dishwashers, visitors, deckhands, and even the Captain, laid into the lines to haul that monster around, only the engine crew being exempt as they were still hard at work in the unbelievable heat of the engine room, trying again to repair the boilers.

After a shower, I put on my cleanest dirty clothes, packed my bags, and said my goodbyes to a bunch of guys that I had really come to like. I gathered a few phone numbers to call for the crew members when I got back to the states, for it cost a fortune to call out of here, thanked them for their hospitality, adopted them as fellow Texans, and headed for the airport.

Chapter Nineteen

(taxi to Dakar airport)

The taxi ride from the hotel to Dakar airport was not something I looked forward to, and sure enough, my misgivings were not misplaced.

Having fought many a verbal pitched battle with these scavengers of the streets, I felt confident of holding my own in what I hoped to be my last ride in a Dakar taxi. This slight feeling of confidence caused me to make my first mistake. I let the driver put my two duffel bags in the trunk. As we pulled away from the curb, I asked why his meter wasn't turned on.

"It's broken," was his reply.

"Stop and let me out," said I.

After a short argument, the driver managed to repair his "broken" meter. "No good," was my response, pointing out that the meter started running with me already owing him a thousand Senegalese francs before we had gone a city block.

"I'll pay two thousand francs for the ride to the airport, no more!" I said.

"No, no, no, airport is five thousand francs!" said the taxicab driver.

"Two thousand, no more!" I said, with a scowl.

He acted mad and sullied up. I sullied up, too, and didn't have to act mad. I was mad!

Then, I realized my mistake.

I had given my opponent, and that's the correct word, a trump card to use against me by allowing him to lock my bags in the trunk. If I had kept the bags forward with me, he would have to be reasonable, or I could walk into the airport without settling with him. As it was, he had my things locked up, and I would have to deal with him. If I got out of the taxi and he wasn't satisfied, he could drive away with my bags. I then decided to stay in the taxi until he got out,

111

and not offer to pay anything until my luggage was safely in my hands.

By the time we reached the airport, his runaway meter read seven thousand francs. I offered three thousand, and you would have thought I had insulted his grandmother by his reaction. It was a standoff, so we both just sat! I wasn't worried as it was four hours 'til my flight left. He was losing money!

Finally, muttering curses in Arabic, he got out and opened the trunk. Throwing my bags onto my shoulder, I offered him three thousand-franc notes, which when he refused to accept them, I dropped them into the trunk. He was screaming for the police as I made my way into the terminal.

Conclusion

At the age of 49, my dad, Dean Meeks set off on the most daring adventure of his life.

While he did not successfully complete the journey, this incredible, courageous man gave it a helluva try. He never had to wonder, "What if?" And had he not gotten hurt so badly back home in Gatesville, he might have made it overseas again for another try.

This has been a story trying to escape my brain for a long time and find its way to the written word. I have pushed it aside a number of times, procrastinated and been distracted with life things, but today I have started writing in earnest.

I have long been afraid of writing, telling myself that I am not a writer, and that I could never measure up to my father's work. I am a "buyer." I buy things to start projects, and then never complete them. This project is too important to let that happen any longer.

Dad was such a great writer I did not think I could do his story justice. But now, my dreams and hopes have pushed away the fear, and it is time to share his wonderful story.

There is so much left unsaid and unwritten about this voyage. I wish dad could fill in all the blanks, but he passed away in 2008, and I did not realize that so much was left unwritten.

There are a few stories of his return trip that I've been able to uncover from family and friends. It has been over thirty years, so many details will have to be left to the imagination, but I'll do the best I can.

One anecdote related by family concerns a time dad was waiting in customs somewhere. He was the only Texan, and there were several Russians, and the Cold War was going on at that time, and there was great animosity between the United States and Russia.

Dad had very little money to his name after the multiple airline ticket price changes in Dakar. So, there he was in this room with the Russians, and they were giving him dirty looks, and he was doing the same to them. Realizing that he was outnumbered, and it might be a long wait, he decided to attempt a little communication.

He pulled some American coins out of his pocket and started showing them to his fellow detainees. After a few minutes, the temperature in the room began to warm a little bit, and it wasn't long before they were sharing their food and drinks with him. For just a little bit, the Iron Curtain came down.

Another story comes from his flight home between London and New York, on People Express Airlines. This was an American low-cost airline which operated between 1981 and 1987. Fares were paid in cash, aboard the aircraft, early in the flight. That being said, when the stewardess came to collect the money from dad, he was about six dollars short. She began to read him the "Riot Act," or gave him a good "tongue-lashing," as Ranzell recalls. She told him, "We are going to let you by this time, but in the future, you had better have the right amount of money to fly."

He assured her there would not be a next time.

There were some gentlemen on that flight who worked at NASA with the Space Shuttle Transoceanic Abort landing crew, and dad had met them in his travels, possibly in Africa. According to Ranzell, dad had taken them out on his sail boat to pass some time. When they got to New York, dad had no money and needed a taxi to another airport to catch his final leg to Texas. These gentlemen loaned him twenty dollars or so. Dad got their address and promised to send the money when he got home, which he did.

When he arrived in Houston, he had a quarter to his name and that was just enough to make a phone call (from a pay phone) to his good friend, C.F., who came and picked him up at the airport, fed him, and took him back to his pickup truck for the drive back to Gatesville, Dodds Creek, and the love of his life, Margaret.

~~~~

Dad eventually made it home all right after all those troubles in Dakar, but unfortunately, he never did make it back to complete his sailing trip across the ocean.

I'm really not sure if he ever even wanted to attempt to retrieve the White Swan. I'm sure he thought about her from time to time, but I believe he got a lot of that desire to sail the world out of his system.

Then, in 1987, he had an accident that would forever put any sailing dreams out of the picture completely.

He was back on the ranch and decided to go just up the road on horseback to visit his good friend, Gene Chitwood. After a nice ride and a good visit, he started the leisurely trip back. He was riding a mare we called the Netherland mare (that was the family name of the people he had acquired her from), and he decided to let her graze on the side of the road. As he was sitting relaxed on her back, she was startled, and she jumped and bucked.

Her head was down, and dad was thrown forward, with nothing to stop his fall. He landed face-first on the ground and broke his neck.

As he later told the story, he knew his neck was broken because he couldn't move, and he couldn't breathe. He said he was lying there, blood running down his face, and he thought it was the end for him. He told us all good-bye, and that he loved us very much. He also had a talk with the Good Lord. He made Him a promise that if he got out of this alive, he would be in the Lord's house every time the doors were opened. You see, he had been away from the Lord for quite some time.

Then, as he lay there, he decided to attempt to swallow air to see if he could force air into his lungs. This worked! His respiratory system began to function, and he was able to breathe again.

About this same time, there was a man driving down the road who saw the horse with a saddle and no bridle – dad had pulled the bridle off as he was thrown – and he knew he needed to be looking for someone in the ditches. He found my dad in the ditch. Dad was able to tell him that he had a broken neck. The man, who I do not know, happened to be a retired ambulance paramedic. He stabilized dad and then went for help.

Some would call it luck – I call it divine intervention – but there was a telephone lineman working on the phone lines nearby, and this man was able to call for an ambulance. Again, for you younger readers, this was in the days before cell phones were widely available.

Dr. Stuckey – a good friend of my parents who went to church with my mom (another divine intervention) – was the doctor assigned to the emergency room that day, and just a couple of years ago, he related this story to me:

He said that when dad got to the hospital, they ran some tests, but could not find the break, and so they needed to transfer him to Scott and White hospital, about 35 miles away. The receiving hospital told them not to transfer without a neck brace, and our small-town hospital did not have one. Dr. Stuckey knew that time was of the importance, so he made a decision to transfer, anyway. He told me that he placed sand bags on both sides of dad's neck, taped and strapped him down to the spinal board, and sent him on to Scott and White.

After more testing, it was determined that dad had broken his C2 (this is the second vertebrae of the neck, directly below the skull), and the doctor told my mother that he had only seen this break on dead people. In the research I have found, most people with a C2 break are left fully paralyzed – such as the actor, Christopher Reeves – or dead. That was not to be the case for our "Superman."

Within a short amount of time, he was able to feel his arms and legs, and after intense therapy and surgery, he was able to walk again. He never regained all the feelings in his hands, and he lived with intense pain and insomnia for many years, but he lived! And, he kept his word to the Lord – he rejoined the church in which he was raised, and he took his mother to church every Sunday.

Dad loved his mother very much, and he devoted the later part of his life in loving caretaking of her. After she could no longer drive, he was her transport, her nurse, her grocery man, and when her eyes failed, and she could no longer read, he read to her every evening. They were both very fond of history, and many great stories were shared during this time.

He visited her three to four times a day, making sure her every need was met. He would carry her three times a week out to my mother's ranch to feed her cows, and they would stop at the local hamburger joint for lunch. He was a great man – they just don't make 'em like that anymore!

To say dad was a great man and never mention mom would be a shame.

What kind of woman must it have taken to capture the heart of this giant of a man? What type of woman stands behind her husband as he goes halfway around the world on a boat? A strong independent woman, that's who.

She won his heart in high school and kept it the rest of their lives. I have never seen a love so strong – two people who not only were married, but who loved deeper than words can express.

When mother developed cancer and died suddenly, dad gave up and died two months later. He just couldn't live without her, and so he didn't. Although losing both your parents within two months was hard, to see him grieve and suffer without her was worse. It almost was a blessing to know that he didn't have to be here long without her.

All my life, I put my dad on a pedestal, and I collided with mom. Sometimes I couldn't understand how dad could love her so much. I just couldn't see it. Then, it was pointed out to me that the reason she and I couldn't get along was because I was just like her.

I used to say that if I was like my mother, then just shoot me! Thank goodness, no one did. Today, it is one of the things I am most proud of – to be like my mother.

When I was in high school, she went to college and obtained her degree. She bought one of her father's ranches and owned her own cattle. Dad ran cattle on his parents' land and mom bought the ranch she was raised on, and she ran her own cattle. She was a true Texan, through and through.

Her parents had ten girls – four died at birth and six lived. They were the Perryman six. Needless to say, with six girls, no boys, and three ranches, someone had to learn to work the cattle. Her father was a hard man, and I know it was not an easy life for her. It was that strong and at times abusive raising that made her who she was – Margaret Lynn, the woman my dad loved.

One thing I know is that mother never strayed from the Lord. She was a devout woman. I may not have liked going to church every Sunday, but she really didn't care – she felt it was her duty to raise us girls in the church, and that she did. Mom never wavered in her faith. That is something she gave to me, and that is what I believe held our family together. Although I, like my dad, drifted away from God, I found my way back home to my roots that mother established.

Even though mom and dad had two different religions, it worked. You see, dad was raised Church of Christ, and mother was raised Catholic, and in the 1950s, those two religions did not mix. When I would ask mom or dad about their wedding, they would never give any information. The only thing that dad said once was, "Anything that could go wrong, did."

It wasn't until after my parents died that I found out a little about their wedding.

Dad had dropped out of college, joined the Army, and was stationed in Germany, before coming home to marry mother and take her to Germany with him.

When he came back to Texas, his mother, Lois, was waiting for him at the train station. Lois had learned photography, and she brought a camera with her, but left it in the car when she went to pick him up. In those days, you didn't lock your car, and someone stole her camera. So, on their wedding day, my grandmother did not have her camera. Someone loaned her a camera, and she took all the wedding photos. The only problem was, it was not her camera, and she did not realize that there was a lens cap on it – so none of the pictures came out.

There also was crying from both sides of the family because of the difference in religions. So, from this rough start came a love that could not be broken. Almost a Romeo and Juliet.

There is one very powerful life lesson I learned in my relationship with my mother, and I will take a chance sharing it. I woke this morning with this story on my mind and felt it must be shared. It really has no connection with "Odyssey of a Texas Sailor," but more relates to my own personal odyssey (epic journey – a life wandering; an eventful voyage).

As I mentioned earlier, there was always conflict between mother and myself, and also my sister. Those two fought more than I did. At one time, I was working with a spiritual mentor, and she suggested that I ask God to show me my mother as He saw her. I was willing and began to pray each day that God would show me my mother as He saw her, not as I saw her.

Boy, did he show me!

I was living in La Porte, Texas, near the Gulf of Mexico, and I was meeting up with my family to attend a cousin's wedding in Bryan, Texas. My sister and parents lived in Gatesville, about 120 miles away, and we all went to the wedding together. Mother and I were going to share a hotel room that night, and my sister and dad were going to go back to Gatesville, since he didn't like to leave his mother or his cows for very long.

Mother had car trouble when she arrived at the church, so after the wedding and a little of the reception, we took my sister, Andrea, and dad back to the car to go home to Gatesville. Dad was going to take mom's car home due to the engine trouble. At this time in life, my sister and I were both finding our way back to our Higher Power and learning to trust in God. So, with that being said, when dad went to start the car, I said, "Let's pray," so my sister and I grabbed hands and started to pray that the car would start.

Mom was saying, "It's dead; it won't start." But lo and behold, after a couple of tries, the car started. My sister and I just laughed. Then again, my mother stated, "It was dead!" To which I replied, "Yes, mother, so was Lazarus!"

Dad and Andrea headed back to Gatesville, and mother and I headed back to the reception. On the way back, mother was telling me how upset she was that my sister no longer took her girls to church. She was really starting to get on my nerves, so in a smart-aleck sort of tone, I said, "Your mother must have drug you to church every Sunday!"

She was quiet for a moment and said, "No, I wasn't allowed to go to church, and when I did sneak off to go, my dad would throw rocks at me when I came home."

119

All of a sudden, God showed me my mother as He saw her! Someone who wanted a relationship with God so much that she would risk the abuse just to go to church. My mother didn't change that day, but I sure did.

~~~~

Dad and my sister had their own special relationship.

Through her ups and downs in life, she leaned on him. He had an easy way of listening to your troubles and helping you come through them. On one such occasion, she was blue about something, and dad had the great idea to fly them out to Terlingua, to the world's largest chili cook-off out in West Texas. So, they loaded up in his Cessna and headed west. I have attached an article in the back of this book where dad gives a detailed account of this harrowing trip – just another example of how life with Dean Meeks was never boring.

We were not rich in the financial sense of the word, but we were the richest when it came to life. Our parents saved up and we took summer and winter vacations. They knew how to stretch a dollar. I think they realized that work without play was no life at all. They realized that spending time with your children and having fun was important. We went skiing in the winters and to the beach or the mountains in the summers.

None of these were luxury vacations by any means, but to me, they were the best! We camped in Colorado, swam in the Great Salt Lakes, picked cherries in Utah, saw Old Faithful in Yellowstone National Park. We looked over the rails of the Royal Gorge Bridge in Colorado, and dad drove our station wagon places no wagon should have gone! We lived on the edge – literally!

I recall one adventure where dad was taking us to see this canyon, and he was taking us down a dirt road – not a well-beaten path. I think he liked to avoid well-beaten paths.

Anyway, we were driving along and then – THE BOTTOM OF THE EARTH DROPPED OUT.

120

I was really hoping we were just going to look at this canyon, but no! Dad started down this narrow road with hairpin, switchback curves – in a STATION WAGON!

With each turn, the nose of our car would hover out over the edge of the road. I think I was about ten or eleven at the time, and for some reason, I thought if I pulled on the door handle hard enough, I could keep the car from rolling over the edge.

Obviously, we didn't roll off the edge, but I sure kissed the ground when we got to the bottom of that canyon. I don't believe the road out was as bad as the road in, because if it was, I'm pretty sure I would not have gotten back in the car.

I really have had an amazing life. I am who I am today because my mom and dad were who they were. What gifts our parents give us, if we care to take a closer look. What gifts I can give to my children and grandchildren, if I take the time to play and pray? What is really important today?

Was it the White Swan that was so important, or the journey and lessons learned? Is it how much money I have saved for an elusive retirement, or teaching the grandkids to ride horses that is important?

When I started this journey to get dad's writings published, I had no idea where it would take me.

I thought I would just type up all his journals, and that would be that. But such has not been the case. As with most things in life, I never can see the big picture.

I have gone on this adventure with him.

I have cried, and I have laughed.

I have felt the desolation as he sailed off his map.

I have felt him along the entire journey.

I feel he is with me now.

~~~~

So, what happened to the White Swan?

Well, let me tell you…

Dad had been working in Gatesville as a school bus driver to bring in a little extra money. This job allowed him the flexibility to tend two ranches, and also keep a close eye on his elderly mother.

So, there he was at the Gatesville's bus barn between routes when he receives a call from the American embassy in Dakar. They wanted to discuss ownership of the White Swan.

It was not every day that calls came in from an American embassy to Gatesville's bus barn. Kinda scary how they can track a person from a boat in Dakar, Africa, to small town Central Texas – at the right time!

From what I can tell, that is when the correspondence between dad and the embassy in Dakar started – you can see the letters in the back of this book.

This was in 1993, eight years after he left the Swan berthed in Dakar's harbor. It was quite surprising that the boat was still in the harbor and had not been stolen long before. Dad never received any other information or money for the Swan, but at least they didn't try to fine him for leaving it there. There was mention of customs duty and harbor fines, but after a few years, he quit looking over his shoulder for the customs officers.

~~~~

Dean Meeks had charisma.

He had a way of making you feel special. When you were in a conversation with him, you felt like there was nowhere he would rather be than with you. He was not distracted or thinking of what he wanted to say – he was engaged. He was listening. He cared. That is a gift.

Many of his friends at the funeral stated that he was their best friend. I think he made us all feel like his best friend. To this day, ten years after his death, when I run into one of his friends, they start telling me stories of things they did with dad. There is a light when people are sharing about some of the mischievous and adventurous things that happened around my dad.

122

One such friend, Bobby Jones, had a long confinement to bed prior to his death, and my sister was his home health nurse. Bobby would relive the stories of their friendship every time she went to see him.

I stopped by once, and he shared about how he knew that dad would be waiting on him in heaven with an electric razor, ready to cut his hair. You see, when dad broke his neck, he was confined to a Circolectric bed for a period of time. This was a circular contraption that dad was strapped upon. They could roll it up and he could look at the ceiling or down where he stared at the floor. (They do not use these beds anymore, but it is worth a look on Google to see the contraption he was in.)

He had four "pins" in the side of his head, with a halo brace fastened in place. His friend, Bobby, came to visit him, and dad told him that he could really use a haircut the next time he came to visit. So, being the good friend he was, Bobby brought his electric razor and commenced to give dad a haircut.

But Bobby got a little too close to the metal pins embedded into dad's head and the vibration of the razor must have been incredibly painful! That became a running joke between the two of them – about daddy one day getting him back, even if it wasn't in this life.

Dad had many friends, and all the nieces and nephews felt very close to him. Our home was welcoming. It was a refuge. In the early seventies, after the dairy closed, dad went to work for the State School for Boys here in Gatesville. He was good with the delinquent boys and often brought them to the ranch to go camping.

One of the strategies he used with these boys to help manage behavior and solve problems was the peer pressure system. Basically, the system was this: when one got out of line, all got in trouble. This worked really well, especially when they came to visit the ranch.

After the State School closed in the mid-seventies, my parents decided to try their hand in the foster care system. At this time, mother was going to college for a social work degree, and dad had the experience with delinquent boys. Those qualifications put us in a situation to get some pretty rough kids. Mom and dad did not start out with just one or two – no, they took on five boys at a time. Talk about some life changing experiences for all involved.

I remember dad saying they were brought to us, and our job was to gentle them down a little before they could be placed in long-term homes.

You see, we were the first stop when kids were initially removed from their home. They would arrive at all hours of the day or night. Mom and dad would get them settled, enrolled in school, and show them what it felt like to be safe and loved. So many were abused physically, but it is the mental abuse that is the hardest to see or treat.

Some of the boys were placed in other homes fairly quickly, and some stayed with us longer. I cannot tell you how many boys came through our home, but I think it was somewhere around thirty or more in a five-year period. It was a difficult five years on our family, but I wouldn't trade it for the world.

As a teenager, I had no idea that there was such abuse and neglect out in our society. It was a real eye-opener for me. I saw how unselfish my parents were. I saw them open their hearts to these children and do whatever it took to help them.

Dad purchased a large handmade wooden table with a long bench down one side to accommodate the new additions to our family. All the boys could sit on the bench to eat. Dad placed a silver dollar in the middle of the table, and instructions were given that it was to stay right there.

One day, the coin was gone and, of course, no one did it. So, dad hooked up the flatbed trailer, equipped each boy with a shovel, and took them all to the creek bed. His instructions were that they had to fill the trailer with creek rock. Nobody was to come home for food or anything until this task was completed, and the dollar was returned. He informed the boys that because someone stole the silver dollar, all of them would be punished.

After dad deposited the boys in the creek with their instructions and tools, he snuck around to the high bank to watch the show. He said there was cussing, fighting, name-calling and rock-throwing.

They were all mad at the thief. In a little bit, they all started shoveling rocks and started filling up the trailer.

Later that day, the silver dollar found its way back to the center of the table, never to leave again.

Most of the boys were never heard from after leaving our home, with the exception of two or three. There is David Smith, who I still talk to frequently and call my brother. He stayed with us almost the entire five years. Another was Eloy, who was adopted and his named changed to David.

It was sometime in the early 2000s when dad came home one day, and someone's car was there. He looked around and didn't find anyone, so he went around the back of the house, and there was a young man and his family looking over the creek banks that our house sits alongside. When dad approached, the young man asked if he knew who he was. Dad thought about it and answered, "Yes, you're Eloy."

Eloy, now David, was driving near Gatesville and took a detour to try to find our home. He wanted to stop by, show his family the home place, and tell my parents thank you. I found his phone number in mom's address book after my parents died, and he sent the most beautiful spray of flowers with the following letter attached:

February 1, 2008

Dear Meeks and friends,

It's with heavy heart that I write to the survivors of two of the greatest influences in my life. I, an orphan, came to know what family should be through the dedication of two great people, such as Margaret and Dean Meeks. They taught me to love without conditions. They taught me that anger was okay when the hurt was too much to bear. They instilled a peace into my torn heart, knowing that I would one day leave to another family. They helped me live to breathe yet another day. They stood for commitment, lasting morale, character, and most of all taught the principle of LOVE. In doing so, they portrayed a heavenly being, one that I would learn to appreciate

125

in the years to come. They were instruments of my Savior, the Lord Jesus Christ. They were the bridge to the next chapters in my new life beliefs. The Meeks served each orphan that shadowed the threshold of their front door with a delicate lifestyle; sensing the needs of each of us as being Special. Treating each and every one of us as one of their own.

Learning that all that is special comes from God, then my condolences to all who have survived the late Margaret and Dean Meeks, because having been a witness to this life's miracle, I know has made each of you a very Special person. May the Lord bless them richly with a huge crown upon their head, and may their ears hear the words that we all want to hear, "Well done, my good and faithful servant."

May God bless each of you and my prayers are with you.

Love,
David Eloy

~~~~

There is one thing I always knew without a doubt – if I needed my dad or mom, they would be there.

When I joined the Air Force and was stationed in England, my dad told me that if I needed him, he would be on the first plane over. I knew he meant it. I believe he would have gotten a ticket on the Concorde, if he had to. The Concorde (a now defunct supersonic airplane) could get you from New York to London in one hour! That is the kind of dad I had. I think the world would be a better place if all our dads were like him.

In 1986, my daughter was born in England, and when she was two months old, we flew home to be stationed in San Antonio. As we arrived at the airport after a long difficult flight with a two-month-old, I could see my dad standing with his face to the glass, peering out into the night as our plane approached.

I was crying. I was home, and my parents were there to meet us and their new granddaughter.

I would love to tell you that my marriage was as strong as theirs. That I stayed married happily ever after, but that is not the facts. I have struggled over my life with failed relationships, and consequences of my poor decision-making. I am happy to say that before my parents died, I had returned to church and cleaned up the wreckage of my past. Also, before they passed, I found – or God found for me – the love of my life, Todd Paige.

Eight months after dad died, Hurricane Ike flooded our home on the coast. We later moved into the house that dad built, and where I was raised. I cannot even begin to tell you all of the wonderful gifts I have received since moving into this home.

Frequently, I have felt both mom and dad's presence here. They both have guided me to things. Mother would often communicate through pictures – of course. Dad mainly comes to me in dreams, he is there when I need him the most.

Mom loved taking pictures. Several months after her death, I was standing in the kitchen and looked over into the spare bedroom, and there was a photo on the floor. It was a picture from the 1960s of her younger sister, Mary. I tried to call Mary and she didn't answer, so I called the youngest sister – Honey Bear, as she is known. When I reached HB, she said that she was on the phone with Mary, and they were talking about mom, and they were so sad. I told her that I believed mama wanted me to tell them she was fine.

I don't know if you believe in life after death, but I do. I believe they have been able to communicate with both myself and my sister. They are alive, not only in my heart, in dad's writings and my memories, but all around.

Writing this story has brought them not only closer to me, but maybe closer to you, too.

I hope you have enjoyed a glimpse into the life of Dean and Margaret Meeks.

What's your next adventure?

A Small Favor to Ask

Thank you for reading this book of memories about a wonderful man. I hope you enjoyed it and found something meaningful, memorable, or inspirational in some way.

Now, please help others who might be interested in reading this once-in-a-lifetime adventure story by taking just a minute to write a review on Amazon. Your reviews mean a great deal to the authors, but more importantly, they really do help readers find this book.

You never know, your review might lead someone to discover something that changes their life for the better.

Go ahead, take a minute now and write that review. Thank you in advance.

To read other books by co-author John H. Clark III, visit his website: https://www.johnhenryiii.com/

About the Author(s)

Drew Paige is a wife, mother, grandmother, rancher, military veteran, and last but not least, a nurse. She currently resides with her husband in the home built by her parents in a small town in central Texas. Life on the ranch includes two dogs, several cats, horses, cows, and a rooster or two.

After serving four years active-duty in the United States Air Force as an Electrical Systems Specialist, Drew earned a Bachelor of Science degree in nursing from Hardin Simmons University in 1992, while serving in the Air Force Reserves. Her Air Force career allowed her to travel to several foreign countries. Stationed in England during her active duty, she was able to travel to Scotland, Germany, France, Belgium, and one NATO exercise in Sicily. As a Reservist, she added Guam to her list of travels.

During her nursing career, she has worked in oncology, home health, and in the surgery area, working both in pre-op and recovery over twenty years. The wonderful world of nursing has allowed her to not only raise her family, but also add a few more countries to her list of travels. In 2014, she traveled to Israel, and two years later, found herself on a wonderful trip to Sweden to visit friends. Multiple cruises to the Caribbean with her husband can be listed among her travels, as well.

Although visiting beautiful places around the world is one of her loves, nothing compares to spending time with family and grandchildren. She enjoys horseback riding, bicycle riding, and any outdoor activity around the ranch.

Publishing her father's works has been a dream, and so now she proudly adds the title of author to her list of accomplishments.

~~~~~

Dean Drew Meeks was born November 14, 1935, in a log cabin on a small dairy farm in central Texas. He remained connected to this plot of land his entire life. Raised by loving parents, he was allowed to explore and follow his dreams. Those dreams were many.

Football was one of his first loves and that led him to a college scholarship at Texas A&M University, where he played under the legendary Coach Paul "Bear" Bryant. After three tough years, he stated "football was no longer fun," and he dropped out of college and joined the U.S. Army. While stationed in Germany as a paratrooper, he again took up football and enjoyed a few more years of "some of the roughest and toughest football" around.

130

Meeks married his high school sweetheart in 1957, and they truly lived happily ever after – one of those storybook romances and a classic example of true love and faithfulness. After Germany and the army, Dean and Margaret settled into their life on the farm, where they raised two daughters and continued a life of hard work and fun.

Flying was another area of interest to Dean, so he took some lessons and bought a small airplane to use on and around the farm. After his girls were grown, he decided he also wanted to learn sailing. So, he bought a sailboat, read some sailing books, and taught himself to sail. This dream lead to the adventure of a lifetime and eventually to the book, "Odyssey of a Texas Sailor."

Dean died January 31, 2008, just two months after his beloved Margaret passed away. Some say he died of a broken heart.

It is impossible to sum up Dean's life in just a few short paragraphs. He was truly larger than life.

~~~~

John Henry Clark lives in a one-stoplight central Texas town with three females: a mostly-blind and highly neurotic mini-dachshund; a beautiful calico cat with an eating disorder; and his wife, the wonderful and beautiful woman who takes care of it all. A graduate of the University of Houston, Clark is an award-winning journalist, author, freelance writer, photographer, musician, artist, and avid golfer who has a dozen published non-fiction books, including his best-seller, *Camino: Laughter and Tears Along Spain's 500-mile Camino de Santiago,* which chronicles two of his three backpacking treks along the historic pilgrimage across northern Spain.

A tireless seeker, researcher and questioner, John has written a number of other fascinating books dealing with the human experience, from tragedies to triumphs and more, including his first published title, *Finding God: An Exploration of Spirituality in America's Heartland.* Recently, he has taken up painting, as well, and enjoys using acrylics to create abstract scenes from nature.

For more on John and his books, along with information on his writing services, visit:

www.johnhenryiii.com;
https://www.facebook.com/depressionbluesforum/
and/or:
https://www.facebook.com/johnclarkbooks/

An Interview with Dean Meeks

(Transcript of an article published December 31, 1995
by The Radio Post newspaper)

Levita's Dean Meeks was a local hero and world traveler, albeit very unique.

GATESVILLE (RP) – When Dean Meeks left Gatesville bound for the gridiron at Texas A&M, most folks around here figured he'd do well. It was, and is surprising to some, however, that besides the football field, he counts parachuting, airplane flying and deep water sailing among his loves and accomplishments. We hope you enjoy this week's Jed Arnett interview with Dean Meeks. We're sure you'll find it funny.

Meek is one thing Dean is not.

By JED ARNETT

Jed: You graduated from high school in Gatesville when?

Dean: 1954.

Jed: Did Gatesville have pretty good football teams back then?

Dean: Yeah, Jerry Sullivan and I have argued for 30 or 40 years about who was the best player, and I just wanted it to be in print, maybe, that I was the better player than him. If it's in print, probably it's true. I just wanted to get that down.

Yeah, we had pretty good teams. We weren't great teams, but we were pretty good teams. We were steady. Probably we had a 7-3 and 8-2 record through two of the high school years. We could have

133

won district in our senior year, but we were declared ineligible. One of the boys rode a bucking bronc and took mounting money, which was $5, so he was declared a professional and we were ineligible.

Jed: Who was that, do you remember?

Dean: Oh, yeah. Norris Sexton. It bothered Norris a long time, but I don't think it bothered anybody else because he was one of our favorites. Besides, he really needed the $5. He didn't come up rich. He came up the hard way – every nickel he got.

He worked for my daddy, delivering milk from morning until afternoon. He ran a route – actually ran from the pickup to the house and back – all over town. Maybe in an hour-and-a-half of work, he'd make 35 or 40 cents. He worked hard for his money, and of course nobody else was making any money, either. It was just the times.

Jed: Who were some of the others?

Dean: Bobby Jones was our quarterback and had been since junior high school, and a good one. We had a big line – Joe Payne, Jamie Erwin. We had a real good solid line with some real light, fast guards. We were real competitive.

The thing I remember about high school – when we would lose, we would never be out of the game until it was over. We were still in the game and had hopes of winning right up until the last whistle blew. That may not tell you we were a great team, but we held our own. We had a bunch that would really scrap.

Lloyd Mitchell was our coach and I put him right up alongside my father as a man. And his wife, Madge, well she's right up there with my mother. They were actually family to us – just as much as our own families. When we weren't with our own families, then we were with them or some others, like Sid Pruitt or L.C. Mc Kamie. We were always in good hands.

If any of us turned out to be any count, they are who should get the credit.

Coach Mitchell had influence far beyond athletics.

I never will forget one time – I must have been a sophomore in high school. The coach had a way of leaning back and looking down his old long Indian nose at you and being real quiet for a long time. It sure made you uncomfortable.

He said something to me, and we were across the dressing room from each other – we were the only two in the dressing room. I didn't quite understand him, so I said, "Huh?"

Well, it got real quiet in there.

It was quiet to start with, but it really got quiet then. He was walking by me and he stopped and stood there a long time. Finally, he turned and started looking down his nose at me and he said, "Huh?"

And I said, "Sir?"

He said, "Do you say 'huh,' to your daddy?"

I said, "No, sir."

Actually, I did regularly say 'huh' to my daddy, but I didn't anymore.

When Coach had a victory celebration, he would eat a pie, a cherry pie, after every winning game. When we lost, he didn't get a pie, and he got real grumpy when he missed his cherry pie.

We ended up usually eating at Meeks' Café, up on the square, and I guess the pies got sold in the mornings to the other teams, when we didn't win.

Jed: Who influenced you to go to A&M?

Dean: There were several.

My FFA mentors, S.L. Adams and Mr. Winchler, were teachers in agriculture class, and they were Aggies, and they were 100-percent, as most are.

Jack Roach influenced me quite a bit into going to A&M. Jack helped me get in down there and did some talking for me. He was one of the mainstays in getting me in down there.

I had a scholarship.

Pat James, one of the coaches, came up here and signed me up. It was just unbelievable to me that anybody would want me. I think my mother felt the same way.

I could have gone to college, anyway, but, really, college meant football to me. I look back now and think that was a mistake, but it was that way at the time.

Jed: Your family had a dairy at the time, so how did you find time for athletics?

Dean: My father was a little bit different from most of the other farmers around here. He didn't put us to work on the farm as much as normal farmers did. This was a business and there were hired men to help with the milking – my dad and maybe two men would milk. We did some of the work, but probably not as much as we should have, so we had time to do what we wanted to do.

Jed: When you got to A&M, Paul "Bear" Bryant was the coach. Was that kind of intimidating to a young kid from Coryell County?

Dean: It was. He was a tough coach to play for – real tough. There are a lot of tough coaches around, but he was one of the toughest ones. Of course, he was just getting started, and probably some of the other kids seemed to be mentally tougher than I was. I could take pretty much anything they could dish out physically, or that would come my way. But, mentally, I don't think I was as tough as some of the other kids.

You were never at ease. You were always in a strain. That was something I had never been into before. In high school, football had been fun. When I left A&M and played in the Army, it was fun. But at A&M, it wasn't fun. It was probably six to eight hours a day of football. Then you had your academics after that, which I wasn't real good at anyway. It was a real chore for me.

Jed: Did you participate in the "Death March in Junction?"

<u>Dean</u>: Well, we participated, but we didn't have the reporters with us.

We were at A&M going through the same thing they were going through at Junction, but no reporters were there. We started out with 120 freshmen on scholarship the first day of fall workouts. In two weeks, we were down to 60. Then it went down to 40-something. I don't know where it went from there, but it got thinned out. There was no limit to the amount of scholarships they could give out at a time. He had collected lots of good talent from Texas football players that year.

<u>Jed</u>: Who were some of those other players there at the time?

<u>Dean</u>: A lot of them have gone on and done fairly well. John Crow, of course, he won the Heisman trophy. A brother-in-law of mine, Jack Pardee, did and still is doing well. Gene Stallings was one of the ends. I played right behind Gene. Murray Trimble was a boy with one arm that could do more than most people with three arms. He was tough. Charlie Kruger was there. He was a young fellow. It seemed like he was a year younger than everybody in our class. He was big and good natured until the ball snapped, and then you better look out. I mean, I've got a lump on my jaw he gave me, and I don't guess it'll ever go away.

Anywhere along the line I would have hated to spend much time in front of Charlie. I remember one game, it was my sophomore year, and I was red-shirted. Charlie was going to play across from somebody at Baylor – big fella, all conference. The Waco paper made the statement that he was an Aggie-eatin' Bear. Big posters came out. They were pasted up in Charlie's dressing area. I think Charlie liked to have killed the guy before the game was over because that really got him up to play, and he was a tough player. A good fellow, too.

Kenneth Hall, from Sugarland, was there as a freshman. I don't know whether he stayed his whole sophomore year or not. They had a rule back then down there that if you missed a practice, you were gone. He pulled out. Then he was one of the few that they let come back and try again, and he pulled out again. There were some serious problems between him and the coaching staff.

Jed: Was he a great talent?

Dean: All you have to do is look at his record to see he was a great talent. On the football field, you could see it. There was a clash of personalities there that happened quite often on that team. The people who stayed were just as physically tough and mentally tough. Some of the boys, like myself, weren't as mentally tough as others, but you took it all. It was just a hard place to play football. Whether or not Coach Bryant broke anybody's spirit, I don't know.

Jed: How did Jack Pardee get into the family?

Dean: I don't really know the story on that. Somebody introduced him to my wife's sister. She was a majorette at TCU at the time. But Jack did come by and ask me my opinion on some things. She is a good girl.

Jed: When you left A&M, you went into the service, is that right?

Dean: I was mad at the world when I left A&M, so I joined the paratroopers. I got into the 82nd Airborne and then the 11th Airborne, in Europe. When I got over there, I found out they really liked football in Europe. The American people in Europe were football starved. So, I spent a couple of years playing over there in the military. Things were fun again. Football was fun again. I really enjoyed playing in the service.

Each locale, or where there was an Army base, they had a football team. Southern Germany had a league. The Air Force was all in a different league. We played amongst each other and had a championship game after the season was over between the different services.

We had real good football teams in Germany. A lot of them were college players. Some were officers, some were drafted. We had players from Notre Dame, Syracuse, players from all over the country.

I played my best football in the service. In high school, I was an end. Of course, we played both directions back then. Through the service, it was the same way. You didn't come off the field. If the ball got fumbled, you stayed out there and played. But in the service, I finally became a receiver because I could catch the ball. I finally learned to catch the ball, I guess is what I'm saying.

I set some records over there and got on the all-Army team in Europe the first year I played. The second year I played, we were a demonstration team in Nuremburg for the coach's clinic.

My wife had gone up there with me, and that morning we got word that Eisenhower was sending us to Lebanon – there was a big fracas going on in Lebanon – Beirut. By that evening, we were in Turkey, parachutes on our backs. The next day, we were in Lebanon, up in the mountains, trying to calm the situation there.

The English went into Damascus and we went into Beirut the same morning. We were over there about three months, I think.

Our old colonel was a devout football fan, so he gathered his football team up after they found out there wasn't going to be a shooting war.

He gathered us up and moved us into a monastery way up in the mountains – a Mennonite monastery. So, we played football morning, noon, and night up there. We wore gym shorts and combat boots. If you've ever been tackled wearing shorts and combat boots, you'd know that's pretty rough.

It was a soccer field and it was packed clay – just like a rock.

We did play a game over there with the Marines. If you know anything about Marines and paratroopers, well, there's quite a rivalry there.

Two of the old colonels got a game up between us and the Marines who were on shore. It was supposed to be flag football. It was played in this big Shimon Field, downtown Beirut. Now, in flag football, you just pull the flag off the runner and the play is over. It didn't turn out that way.

I believe it was the roughest game of football I was ever in.

It was full-speed football with no pads, no shirts, and nothing on your knees. When you went down, you lost about half your skin. But I think we finally beat the Marines, thank goodness. Just by one point.

Three different times, our colonel sneaked us down to the airfield and tried to get the football team back to Germany, because he knew he had a good team. But somebody would catch him, and he'd have to take us back. We finally got back to Germany and the regular season was over. They'd already established a European champion, which was the Berlin Bears.

But our colonel got us a game with, I believe, the Stuttgart Stallions, the Southern Germany champions. We beat them 65-6.

Then the Air Force champions accepted a challenge from us and we beat them 50-something to 0.

Then, the Northern Germany champions played us, and we beat them in the 50s and they didn't score. We ended up playing three games and scoring 155 points, and the opponents scored once on us. I don't know how that happened.

We were hungry. We wanted to play football.

Jed: Was the service your introduction to flying?

Dean: Right after World War II, there was a little flying went on west of Gatesville at the old Scott's Airfield, and every time we could scrape $4 or $5 together, we'd go out and fly those planes.

After I got home from the service, I went to Dallas and tried to become an airline pilot. I found out you had to have several thousand flying hours, and it would have taken a lot of money to be a pilot. They were getting all of their pilots out of the service, which was good for those pilots and bad for me. I ended up working for American Airlines for a couple of years – getting my pilots' license, and then coming back here into the dairy business.

I'd bought a little Cessna 120, which is a little tail-dragger. It had a tail wheel instead of a nose wheel. It was built in 1946. But it was the most forgiving airplane you could get in. Anything you'd do wrong, it would correct for you, thank goodness.

My daughter and I used to fly it to Terlingua for the chili cookoff. We got into a storm over Brownwood – the same storm that Billy Nichols was killed in. Billy was a Gatesville boy, I believe a dentist. He was killed in the same storm, I believe, flying up from somewhere in south Texas. He was killed in that storm, and it took them six or eight months to locate the wreck.

Anyway, we ran into the same storm at Brownwood. It was so bad you could hear the rivets popping on the airplane. There wasn't anything to do but just fly through it. You'd go up for a while and down for a while – then sideways.

An interesting part – when we got to Terlingua, the airfield down there was a dog-leg. It didn't go straight. It went up a ways, and it turned. So, to land or take off, you had to get up enough speed just so you could get around that curve and then take off. On the way back, as we got off the ground up there, maybe 300-400 feet, my daughter said, "Daddy, I think we've got a problem here."

I said, "What's wrong?"

She said. "We're losing gas."

So, I looked, and sure enough, the sump drain had come unscrewed and fell out. There was a stream of gas coming out of the wing about the size of your finger.

So, I said, "Andrea, open the door, lean out, and stick your finger in the hole."

She was young and did it.

She leaned out and stuck her finger in the hole. I had to get enough altitude to be able to turn around and land. She got out still with her finger in the gas tank, and I went and cut a piece of sage brush, stuck it in there as a stopper, and we came on home.

That might be the last time she has done what I told her.

Jed: You never have landed on the Levita Road, have you?

Dean: Well, a time or two, but I always have somebody up there to flag traffic.

I'll never forget one time I took off headed up the Levita Road from my house. Jack Patton was supposed to be up there flagging traffic, and I had told him to stand in the road when there was no traffic. He was standing in the road, and when the plane got off the ground, it began to sputter. It would catch and then sputter some more. Finally, Jack couldn't stay in the road anymore, and he took off.

He met me at the airfield when I got there, and he said, "I tried to stay in the middle of the road, but that just looked awful."

I said, "You think it looked awful from where you were at, you ought to have been where I was!"

Jed: You tried to sail across the Atlantic once. What motivated that?

Dean: Well, my younger daughter, Drew, had gotten in the Air Force and was stationed at Mildenhall, England. That was my chance to go to England, so I went and visited her there. I got to bumming around England a little, and I had always loved boats of any kind – anything that would float. Anywhere from floating down Dodds Creek to getting on the ferry at Galveston – I loved them all.

I would go out and spend my day looking at boats. I ended up bidding on a boat that was for sale. I didn't think I'd get it, but I bid on it. Later on, I found out I'd bought it. I either had to sail it or sell it.

I had sailed a little on Lake Belton. It's similar to the Atlantic – it's wet. But there's very little tide on Lake Belton, and I found out tides are a big part of an ocean.

We got caught in the middle of a river when my daughter and I were learning to sail this boat in England. She's been around me a long time. She knew I was crazy.

We got caught on this river, and the tide was going out. When the tide goes out over there, it goes out in a hurry, and it goes out a bunch. In a period of about 30 minutes, we had been grounded, and the boat was over on its side. There was no water left, just a river of mud. It was 12 hours between tides, so we had a 12-hour wait until the tide came back in. We spent the night laying on the bulkhead, and every now and then, somebody would start giggling.

All night long, they'd giggle. My daughter, her husband, and I were there. I said, "You may forget a lot of things in your life, but you'll always remember where you were tonight."

The next morning, we pulled her off with the anchor, got back in the stream, and headed back to port. This was about 1985 – somewhere in there – in the summer ... early summer, I guess.

One morning, I just slipped my lines and headed out without my paperwork. Come to find out I was on the high seas. In some ports, I didn't have to have paperwork to get in, and while they were arguing, I'd just pull up my anchor and go. Nobody ever chased me, but it was a strange situation.

<u>Jed</u>: What course did you take?

<u>Dean</u>: I intended to go down the coast of Spain and France, Portugal, across to Africa, and out to the Canary Islands. It was similar to the course that Columbus had taken. I figured if he had done it, it had to be all right. The English Channel was something I hadn't counted on. It was fog. Sometimes you could see three feet; sometimes you couldn't see the front of your own boat. You'd hear the big ships with their fog horns, and you knew they were close, but you didn't know where they were. I spent two days lost on the English coast in the fog.

One time, the tide carried me up the Thames River. I was nearly to London, and I thought I was nearly to France. So, I asked a lady on a pier as I sailed by, "Where am I?"

She said, "On the Thames, in England."

I said, "Thank you, but this is not where I'm supposed to be."

I went by myself. When you're by yourself and you make some big mistakes, there's nobody looking over your shoulder. The main reason was, I didn't want to put anybody else in danger. I don't mind putting myself in a bad position, because a lot of times you can get yourself out. But when you have somebody else to take care of, it's a different situation.

So, when I got down to Guernsey and Jersey, a couple of islands off the coast of France, I spent a couple of days there with

143

the crews of some tall ships. They come in there every year. So, I befriended some sailors there and they taught me some things – they even helped me buy some equipment to help with coastal navigation down the western side of Europe.

Jed: Did those experienced seamen think you were nuts?

Dean: Probably so, but after they learned I was from Texas, they kind of accepted that.

They were a very friendly bunch, and the thing about sea people is they're a lot like cowboys. If you're one of them, you're usually accepted, and they'd do anything for you. So, I was aboard their ships, and they treated me just like one of them. I'd read all my life about the old sailing ships, and I'd always wanted to climb the mast of a tall ship and go out on the yardarms, like the early sailors did.

There was a girl about 60-foot up on a rope swing, working on one of the masts. She asked if I wanted to come up, so I climbed, and I climbed, and I climbed. So, she said, "Now that you're up here, would you mind going out to the end of the yard and get me that rope?" I think she just wanted to see if I'd go out there. I wanted to see if I'd go out there, too.

It was about 60 feet down to the deck, and I kept thinking in my mind that old-time sailors had to do this in the storm, in the dark. It was a chore to go out there and get the rope.

After I went around the eastern tip of France, the weather became better. The sun came out, and the water turned green. It was beautiful from there to Spain.

One day, a whale came up behind the boat. It was a black-and-white killer whale. He went back down, and the next time he came up, there were several behind him. The next time he came up there were 50-60 behind him. They were in a "V-shape," and my boat was the point. By the time they were through, there were several hundred of them back there in a big "V." They were using me as a point. I guess they were just curious. It was a beautiful sight. They would all come up at the same time and stay up about thirty seconds. After about six or eight trips up, they all went down, and I never saw them again.

Somehow, it seems like that should have scared me, but it didn't. It was one of those things that I didn't pay for, but I got anyway.

I'd sailed over to the coast of France and I wasn't a good enough sailor to head into a wind. I ended up over on Omaha Beach, where the Americans went ashore during D-Day, in World War II. I was trying to get around the point, but the wind and tide was keeping me back. I anchored for the night.

At midnight, the tide went the other way, and I got my anchor and my sails up. I could hear a roar ahead of me, and I knew where I was. There wasn't supposed to be any roar there. I tried to sail away from it, but the tide was carrying me right into it. It was a wall of water about six-foot tall. It just stayed in place and broke continuously. It looked terrible. All I could do was head into it and go through it. The water came all in the boat. It was what they called overfalls, where water is coming together from two big bays. One is higher than the other, and the one I was in was the bottom one. I'd never heard of that, but I've seen it now.

While in the Canaries, I ran into this Danish sailor, and we got to talking. He wanted to know what I was doing, and I told him.

He said, "Well, you can make it in that boat."

I said, "Well, I'm glad."

He'd spent 30 years sailing for Mobil Oil, sailing these big tankers. He said, "When are you going, in January?"

I said, "No. It's August, and I'm going now."

He said, "Well, you can't go now. It's hurricane season, and you'll meet at least three between here and America."

I said, "Well, I don't have any choice. I'm out of food, and I'm out of money"

He said, "You do have a choice. You can stay here for a while and do all right, then go. Or you can go now and drown. If you choose to go now, it's been nice knowing you."

He was an old sailor, and I had learned by then to listen to old sailors. That always worried me a little bit, so I changed my plans

145

and headed down the coast of Africa a little bit, instead of coming straight across.

I picked up an English boy and he was not a sailor. When we'd get in bad weather, he'd go below, get in bed, and put a pillow over his head. He was not an asset.

In Senegal, in Dakar, I'd made good friends with some sailors there. One night, I couldn't get back into the marina where I'd been anchoring. I'd taken some of the crew on sails – they were more-or-less ship bound. The marina was too shallow to go into except at high tide. I anchored about a quarter-mile off this beach, where there was a restaurant and a bar there. The four or five men that were with me, we swam in. We stayed there until the bar closed, and the other men just walked back to their ship, which was about two miles around the coast. I had to stay there until midnight to get into the marina.

At about 10:30 that night, I decided to swim back to my boat, except I couldn't see my boat anymore. It was out there in the dark. That morning, we had seen about two big tiger sharks that off-shore fishermen had brought in. The natives just hate a shark. They'd take spears and stab him – all sorts of things. So, as I swam back to my boat, all I could think of was sharks. Of course, they are nocturnal feeders, and there I am splashing along in the dark. So, I began to swim quietly and try to locate my boat. There was a Russian fishing fleet anchored about five miles out. When I could skylight my boat against the lights of that fishing fleet, I could locate my boat.

I began to hear the music from "Jaws." I could just feel these sharks nipping at my heels. When I got about 10 yards from my boat, I put on all the speed I had, and I went over the side of that boat like a scared rabbit.

One time, we were anchored off the coast of Morocco, and I swam ashore to talk to a shepherd to see if I could determine exactly where we were. The tide was going out, and it was a strong current. I got ashore OK, but when I tried to talk to the Arab, he knew no English, and I knew no Arabic. But we were friendly enough. To get back to the boat, I went up the beach about 200 yards because I didn't want to get washed past my boat and out into the sea. That would have been the end, I guess.

146

As I said, the English boy was no sailor, and I don't know if he'd been able to get the boat under way to help me out. When I finally got close, I could tell I wasn't going to get to the boat. So, I started yelling at him to throw me a line. He got a line and threw it to me, and I caught it and got aboard.

I didn't think about it until later, but when I realized what I had done, I decided it wasn't a smart thing to do. If it hadn't been for him, I'd have been in trouble.

He earned his passage right there.

Letters

September 22, 1993

Ismael Sidiby
Inspecteur Principal
Senegal Customs Director
Dakar Port
Dakar, Senegal

Dear Sir:

I am sending this letter via the U.S. consul in Dakar to your attention sir in the sincere hop that you may be of some assistance to me. I am the owner of a 30 foot sailboat "The White Swan" which I had to leave in Dakar in 1985 due to a family emergency which compelled me to travel without delay back to the United States.

I have never been able to return to Senegal to repossess my boat and remain unable to return due to failing health. I have indicated to the United States Consul at our Embassy that I would like Mr. Bassinet of the Marina to sell the boat as expeditiously as possible. I have sent a power of attorney to that effect as well. I would appreciate your every assistance in this matter sir and would simply like to settle this affair. Please contact either Mr. Bassinet of the Marina or the U.S. Vice Consul, P.P. Declan Byrne at the U.S. Embassy if anything further is required of me. I am

Sincerely Yours,

Dean Meeks

Translation of Customs letter.

I am in receipt of letter forwarding Mr Dean Meeks' letter in which he was requesting an authorization to have Mr Bassinet sell the sailboat lying at the Hann bay since 1985.

I would like to draw your attention to the fact that as soon as the investigation started, Mr Bassinet, acting as the owner requested us to get in touch with Mr Feeney and Mr Shekmer who were representing Mr Meeks's interest in Senegal. Once we have been in touch with Mr Shekmer and Mr Feeney, they were given a 4 month deadline followed by several follow-up letters to obtain enough information to prove the regularity of the entry of the boat in Senegal. The section 207 of the Customs code stipulates that all proofs should be submitted at the first request of the service. Under these circumstances it has been retained an offence qualified as smuggling which is condemned by the section 310 and 309 of the customs code.

Therefore a report has been drafted in front of Mr Bassinet who disclaimed responsability in this matter. On top of that the President of the Tribunal Hors Classe of Dakar has ordered on May 24 1993, on the request of the Customs Administration the seizure of the boat which will be sold by auction in the benefit of the Customs Administration.

I regret to inform you that a favourable answer cannot be reserved to your request and to Mr Meeks' request which unfortunately reached us too late.

Embassy of the United States of America

Dakar, Senegal
December 3, 1993

P.P. Declan Byrne
Vice Consul
American Embassy Dakar
Senegal, West Africa

Dean D. Meeks
Rt. 3, Box 381
Gatesville TX 76528

Dear Mr. Meeks:

I regret to inform you that we have had final word concerning the disposition of the The White Swan. I have attached the letter we received from the Customs Service explaining very clearly their position. I have translated their letter for you into English.

Essentially, due to the length of time that has passed since the boat was first berthed in Dakar, the Customs Service is impounding the boat in an attempt to recuperate customs duty and harbor fines. They will auction it and apply the proceeds to the owed duty. I am assured that this will at least exonerate you from any further liability in this manner.

I am sorry this communication could not have been more positive. Please do not hesitate to contact me if you have any further questions.

Sincerely,

P.P. Declan Byrne

For more pictures, please visit:
OdysseyofaTexasSailor.com

150

To read more works published by
johnclarkbooks, visit:
<u>www.johnhenryiii.com/my-books</u>.

johnclarkbooks

Made in the USA
Lexington, KY
08 January 2019